D1319108

BeAttitudes
f o r   w o m e n

Wisdom from Heaven
for Life on Earth

BeAttitudes
f o r   w o m e n

Wisdom from Heaven
for Life on Earth

DOROTHY KELLEY
PATTERSON

WIPF & STOCK · Eugene, Oregon

Wipf and Stock Publishers
199 W 8th Ave, Suite 3
Eugene, OR 97401

BeAttitudes for Women
Wisdoms from Heaven for Life on Earth
Copyright©2000 Dorothy Kelley Patterson
ISBN 13: 978-1-60608-012-2
Publication date 9/1/2008
Previously published by Broadman & Holman Publishers, 2000

Dedication

to those who bring happiness to me

To the parents who have provided a sure heritage:
Charles and Doris Kelley
T. A. and Roberta Patterson

To the sisters and brothers whose fellowship continues:
David and Rima Amad
Kathy Kelley
Russell and Charlene Kaemmerling
Chuck and Rhonda Kelley
Steve and Eileen Turrentine

To the nieces and nephews whose happy visits I anticipate:
Beth, Angie, Perry, Kelley, and Claire Kaemmerling
Sarah Turrentine
Yaser and Nadia Amad
and now many grand-nieces and grand-nephews

To the husband, children, and grandchildren
who bring me great joy and delight:
Husband Paige is my provider, protector, leader,
mentor, lover, and best friend.
Son Armour Paige is my firstborn and encourager and fellow-author
and Daughter-in-love Rachel.
Son-in-love Mark Anthony and Daughter Carmen Leigh Howell
are following our path to kingdom ministries.

Granddaughters Abigail Leigh and Rebekah Elizabeth
give me hope for another generation of godly seed.

Mina, with her children Negina and Nasrullo,
from Afghanistan often join our family circle.

Contents

Preface

In determining how the Christian life is to be lived, no standard is more important, for women or men, than the Bible. How do you approach the Bible? Is it your ultimate handbook for living? Is it your final authority? Is it your primary source for learning about God and the life He challenges you to live? Does the Bible stand above your own subjective, mystical experiences? Does the Bible set your boundaries for Spirit-led decision-making?

Merely reading the Bible, even if you do so in a systematic manner and on a daily basis, is not enough. Superficiality, especially in spiritual matters, is devastating. To meditate upon the principles found in God's Word and to appropriate them wisely in life are essential disciplines if the Bible is to be your light and guide for Christian living. To refuse to accept Scripture as authoritative in your life is irresponsible.

You should not come to the Bible with the intent of reading into its text your own conclusions. In a sense you can prove anything from the Bible. That is how heresies develop. Women and men propagating heresies are more often mistaken than dishonest. Most are sincere. Their innovative theories spring from personal experience and preferences. These theories are then injected into the

Bible until finally, at least in their own eyes, the theories embraced seem to appear on every page. You must avoid allowing your own personal experience to be the lens through which you interpret what God is saying in His Word.

On the other hand, when you come reverently to the text of Scripture, seeking to understand what the text means and how it affects your life, you will find that deciphering its meaning and implementing its teachings will go far beyond your own resources. I have given much of my life to theological studies. I began with three graduate academic degrees in theology; I have continued to use the tools gleaned from theological training to translate and study the Scripture for myself and to find better ways to teach the Bible to women. I have prepared this *interactive devotional commentary* as a tool for women to use in studying and understanding the text of Scripture.

This volume is designed to provide a resource for studying a portion of the Sermon on the Mount—what has been identified over the centuries as "the Beatitudes."[1] Brief and readable *commentary* sections explain the text, including key word studies, grammatical notes,[2] historical allusions, and explanatory information. The *devotional* element offers practical applications from my own five-plus decades of living in a family and ministering to women, together with inspirational quotations (especially from other women), hymns, poems, and vignettes from the lives of biblical characters. The *interactive* portion gives the reader an opportunity

1. Matt 5:3–12.

2. Note that pronouns referring to deity are capitalized. This option not only expresses in linguistic style awe and respect for the Lord but also erases any hint of the anti-supernatural bias that has invaded modern literature. This policy is consistent with quotations from the New King James Version of the Bible. It also adds clarity by helping the reader easily identify antecedents for pronouns.

to study maps, to work through appropriate charts, and to meditate introspectively on what the text is saying. Many biblical references are found in the footnotes to give you the option of reading exactly what the Bible says. Your interaction with the Bible also helps you to appropriate what you have learned from the text into your own life.

God has spoken through His Word to women in every generation with the same clarity and authority with which He revealed Himself to the women of the Bible. The timeless principles of Scripture begin by molding character and are then to be applied appropriately to everyday life generation by generation.

These guidelines for life surpass all other human wisdom for living a productive life. Those to whom its message is directed are promised blessings to be received, but they are also given commands by which they are to order their lives. These principles are far more than rules for a future millennial kingdom. Though general in character, they arise out of the nature of God Himself, and they are based on the reality of truth and morality from God's perspective.

The Beatitudes first and foremost paint a portrait of Jesus. In this self-portrait, Jesus Himself embodies each quality. He then points to Himself because there is no one else who so perfectly portrays the wonderful qualities described. As you hear Him speak from the text of Scripture, you are invited to go where He has already gone and to do what He has already done. You are challenged to imitate Him.

The Beatitudes are also to form the canvas on which a portrait of the Christian is to be drawn. They describe what the Lord expects the citizens of His kingdom to be. Both the commandments of Moses and the Beatitudes of Jesus are expressions of accumulated wisdom that raise a standard above what the world would expect. Despite the similarities, the two ethical treatises are marked by decided differences. Moses attributes goodness to the performance of certain deeds, and he does so in a negative sense; i.e., you are good by refraining from doing certain tasks.[3] Jesus, on the other hand, makes no reference to deeds. He refers instead to the qualities of the heart as determining who is righteous.[4] As you move through your own life pilgrimage to reap happiness and experience the blessings of heaven, may God grant an open heart, a willing spirit, and an eager mind to help you along the way!

An Addendum of Personal Gratitude

My husband was serving as president of Southeastern Baptist Theological Seminary in Wake Forest, NC, during the writing of the initial manuscript. I am indebted to SEBTS and especially to the staff in the President's home, Magnolia Hill. Jan Gold, Bobbi Moosbrugger, and Diane King carried extra burdens in order to enable me to give my attention to the research and writing. Terese Jerose tracked down illusive sources in the library. Dawn Jones and Chris Thompson in the President's Office helped with charts and footnotes. Editor Len Goss patiently gave my work refinement.

In preparing to reissue the volume, I am indebted to our Southwestern Baptist Theological Seminary family. When my husband assumed this presidency, we made the move to Fort Worth, Texas. Here again I am able to do research, write, and teach because of the excellent partners God has given us in ministry. Jason Duesing, Chief of Staff, oversees a capable group—Chris Johnson and others in the president's office; my administrative assistant Candi Finch, researcher Tamra Hernandez, interns Justin Williams

3. Ex 20:3–17.
4. Matt 6:19–21.

and Preston Atwood, and the hospitality team directed by April DeVenny here at Pecan Manor. The tribute to my family is found in the Dedication. Humanly speaking, they are the central focus of my life. They fuel my creativity, provide illustrative material that actually happened, and love me even when I am deeply engrossed in a project!

—Dorothy Kelley Patterson
Pecan Manor
Fort Worth, Texas
July 2008

Introduction

Inside-Out Attitudes

President Theodore Roosevelt experienced a teachable moment through a life-changing incident. What he had always considered a burden became to him in a moment a life-saving blessing. Before the invention of bifocals, someone as near-sighted as the president had to carry two pairs of glasses—one for near vision and another for vision far away.

When visiting the city of Milwaukee, Roosevelt was shot by a man named Schrenk. The surgeon who treated the president after the attempted assassination handed Roosevelt his steel spectacle case. According to the physician, the presence of this bulky case in his pocket had saved the president's life by breaking the force of the bullet and thereby deflecting the deadly shot from his heart.

Accepting the case with its shattered spectacles, Roosevelt remarked, "Well, I've always considered the burden and handicap of having to carry those two pairs of glasses, especially these heavy ones that were in this case, as a very sore one, and here at last they have been the means of saving my life."

All You're Meant to Be

All you're meant to be should inspire you to be all. Believers in Christ are required to live a certain way. My good friend Mary

Crowley used to say that living the Christian life is not so much doing certain things as it is acknowledging that there is a certain way of doing everything! Suddenly all you are and have become are His, and thus they are no longer yours. Certainly such an overwhelming challenge calls for a general attitude of obedience and for the recognition that selflessness is a biblical virtue.

In the Beatitudes, Jesus presented character traits that would become the foundation for successful and godly living. The Beatitudes recorded in Matthew 5:1–12 and those found throughout the rest of Scripture are usually expressed in the third person. Each consists of a blessing, a description of the recipient of this blessing, and an unveiling of the attitude or behavior that would prompt the blessing.

The Beatitudes are not meant to be merely an ethical code or moral system, nor are they a new set of rules and regulations to be viewed as the New Testament's version of the "Ten Commandments." Rather these verses describe the qualities that are to characterize believers. However, they are not natural qualities, even for believers. No one is born exhibiting these unusual characteristics.

A picture is given of the believer as God planned her to be. Since you can escape from everyone but yourself, living with yourself is by far your greatest adventure and most pressing challenge. A look at the Beatitudes will turn your attention inward. Taking these principles seriously will refashion your innermost being into what pleases the Father and brings genuine joy to you.

These qualities are produced only by God's grace. An individual's natural temperament or personal unique nature can be governed to some extent through self-determination, but the character qualities prescribed for the Christian life are not attained according to genetic code or natural bent. Rather, the power of the gospel lies in its ability to take any woman and transform her. through the work of the Spirit of God, from the inside out into what God meant her to be.[1]

Without Christ you are placing your confidence in your own abilities, but with Christ you recognize your limitations.[2] You are able to move from developing a confidence in your own self-image to accepting a commitment to mold yourself as closely as you can into the God-image in which you were created.[3] Your self-confidence, self-expression, and self-control should evolve into confidence in God, in reliance upon the expression of God's presence in your life, and in a willingness to put yourself under God's control, even in the most mundane decisions you have to make.

A Thought to Consider

Attitude, an inward feeling expressed by outward behavior, can be observed even when words are not spoken. What you are on the inside has more impact on your emotional state than the circumstances on the outside (see Prov. 15:13–15).

Most of the Beatitudes are found in the Bible's Wisdom Literature, though they are also sprinkled throughout the Old Testament (see the Old Testament Beatitudes chart on pages 41–42 and the Beatitudes in the Psalms chart on page 43). However, the most famous listing is found in the New Testament in the heart of the Sermon on the Mount (see Beatitudes for Women chart on page 48).

The Beatitudes are not meant just to portray rewards for a prosperous future or prophecies for a blissful heaven. Rather, primarily they are affirmations of what happens to the Christian who lives the Spirit-filled life and claims the by-products of such a life. Obviously, there is a huge gap between the lifestyle God challenges believers to live, which is patterned after the life of Christ and explicitly described in the Bible, and the lifestyle that one who is marred by human

frailties is actually living in a sinful world. In other words, the
Beatitudes present a general description of God's woman. They project
a lofty ideal of Christlike living.

Jesus assumed that every Christian woman would have the seed
that produces the fragrant blossoms of these qualities set forth in the
Beatitudes. However, these godly, perfect ideals are truly a glass ceil-
ing that inevitably shatters under the bombardment of the behavior of
imperfect human beings. Even Christian leaders find themselves willing to talk with gusto and to write with rhetorical excess about these
disciplines of the Christian life more than they are willing to expend
energies and creativity in practicing these principles. Philip Yancey
calls this impasse the "twang of dissonance" in which believers vainly
strive for ideals they know will never be attained in this life.[4]

Of course, you must not assume that the development and smooth
functioning of all or any of these character qualities is prerequisite to
your salvation. Nor should you approach these godly disciplines as you
would a cafeteria line from which you can pick and choose whatever
suits your fancy. Rather, you should not be satisfied until these traits
are continually being sought and developed in your own life. The
wholeness of God's blueprint for the Christian life must come into view
in order to understand properly any one of the particular injunctions
suggested for living that life.

Though the truths Jesus set forth in the Sermon on the Mount are
repeated many times in Scripture, the sermon itself is a uniquely comprehensive statement of the moral principles Jesus believed to be
essential for kingdom citizenship. Obviously Jesus presented His sermon expecting immediate responses from His hearers.

The Beatitudes are not a dated collection of lofty principles to
ponder passively, but rather they are timeless instructions in daily living to be pursued actively. Certainly Jesus must have been concerned
about counteracting the earthly views of the religious leaders of His
day. This concern and the comprehensive way in which Jesus made

the presentation could explain the placing of this strategic sermon early in Matthew's Gospel and the suggestion by some that Jesus delivered the same sermon to different groups.[5]

A Woman's Wisdom

"There are two things to do about the Gospel—
believe it and behave it."

—Susanna Wesley

No one can live out the Sermon on the Mount without the enabling power of Christ within. No measure of self-discipline is adequate to live up to this awesome standard. Human efforts toward perfection are doomed to end in disappointment. However, the Beatitudes present a standard that is described elsewhere in the New Testament as the "new commandment."[6] Believers are admonished to love one another even as Christ loves them. The Sermon on the Mount describes how we are to do this Christlike loving.

Not only do these Beatitudes tell you how to live, but they also point you back to the gospel and the grace that delivered this gospel. The deliverance promised in the gospel of Jesus Christ will draw you like the warmth of the fire's flame. You then must choose whether to be consumed by the flame because of your concern with personal inadequacy or to seize the flame as a torch to light life's path.[7]

Moving Against the Tide

The Christian life is an upstream flight, which, if pursued in your own strength, could end in moral and spiritual exhaustion. But in Christ, moving against the tide serves to strengthen and build up, enabling you to experience growth and refinement by moving toward Him and in His way.

Studying this sermon more than anything else will drive you to see your ultimate need of salvation and remind you of the unmerited favor with which such grace was delivered through the atonement of Christ. As the Beatitudes underscore personal helplessness, and in so doing seem to crush you, Christ is there to lead you into that blessed state in which you are no longer driven by your own desires. Rather, you are able to live your life filled with His life and renewed with His mind. This will lead to glorious happiness.[8]

The Sermon on the Mount is not a scheme for self-improvement or a paradigm for pseudo-perfection. Rather, its principles present a direct road to blessing as God penetrates this fallen world. In so doing, He enables you as a believer to experience challenging demands, through which you will be drawn to the discipline necessary for Christlike living.[9] As you sense your own inadequacy, you will seize the promise of God's grace to lead you beyond your personal frailties.

A Woman's Wisdom

"Jesus says that any reform that starts on the outside and works in is beginning at the wrong end. Christ starts on the inside and works out. The only way of getting a good life is first getting a good heart."

—Henrietta C. Mears

What a Sermon!

Somewhere in Galilee there was a setting that became a vast outdoor auditorium in which Jesus delivered this awesome sermon. As you visualize what kind of area this would have been, you might want to scan the map on page 11 for possibilities.

The sermon was delivered deliberately and with logical sequence. Each phrase in this composite picture accentuates a distinct spiritual feature. As certain principles are presented, others follow on the basis of the previous ones. The comparison is to be with the whole portrait—uniting all the parts, each with its own beauty and utility—making up a kingdom citizen.

The Sermon is delivered especially to believers. Although unbelievers could also profit from its message, they are unable to understand the essence of true happiness and blessedness, since such paradoxes would be so far beyond their understanding that they would appear to be hidden. Those living in the mold of the world would hold that an abundance of possessions and luxurious comforts are indispensable to contentment and happiness.[10]

Interestingly, Jesus did not present His specifications on what a Christian ought to be to His inner circle of apostles, nor did He seem to be aiming merely at the multitude of seekers in general. Rather, Jesus seemed to direct His message to those who were poor, hungry, weary, afflicted, and especially to those who acknowledged their own needs and yearned for comfort.

There is no hint by Jesus that these character qualities result from natural tendencies. Each is produced by grace alone through the working of the Holy Spirit within the human heart. Each builds upon the previous one and presupposes the one to come. A deep chasm that cannot be crossed lies between the spiritual qualities described here and the pseudo-human qualities that appear alongside them.

For example, a woman who appears humble because of her natural temperament to withdraw and her unfortunate circumstances of poverty in life is not automatically "poor in spirit." In looking for an understanding of these characteristics described by the Lord, you must be quick to understand that you are not looking for anything natural. Rather, your search is for a quality that is produced by grace. All of us, regardless of circumstances of birth or natural disposition of temperament, are challenged to reach out for this Christlike way of living that is within the reach of everyone.

The world has continued to come into the church, and the church has continued to become more worldly. What was acceptable only in the world twenty-five years ago is now acceptable in the church. Yet believers must still look for ways to draw a clear distinction between the church and the world. The characteristics described in the Beatitudes are points of reference for determining the basic and essential differences between the believer and the nonbeliever.

Only when the believing woman is absolutely different from the woman of the world does she attract the attention of nonbelievers so that they are willing to listen to her message. Christians dare not seek to be more like non-Christians. Rather, they should desire to be more like the Christ, whose name they bear. As they become more like Him, they are more unlike those who are not Christians.

An Incurable Condition

This condition called "blessedness" is offered by God. It includes all the good you could hope to achieve and much more; it is a permanent joy that is not affected by the ups and downs of life.

On a visit to Rome, I paused at the foot of the Scala Santa in the midst of the crowd of pilgrims, most of whom were ordinary women just like me—daughters, wives, mothers, each with her own burden or heartache and each with a prayer on her lips. They came to this sacred stairway to secure divine favor and achieve some measure of happiness. Usually they ascended on their knees, which were often scarred and bleeding by the time they reached the top.

How I ached to communicate to these women that the ritual of climbing these steps would bring healthy exercise and, in the process, could produce physical pain; but even such a challenging endeavor would never bring them spiritual satisfaction. How my heart wanted to invite them to commit themselves to Christ and then to ascend some much more promising steps, which also would require discipline and commitment but would in the process bring ultimate peace and joy.

The steps upon this earth that lead to the summit of heavenly blessedness are clearly marked in the Beatitudes. They will cause you to stretch yourself to growth, maturity, and a resurrection of the qualities God's Spirit wants to nurture within every believer.

As the blessed controller of all things, the Lord will never abandon His children. Though He may lift His hand for a time to permit you to walk through a dark valley, He is always there in the shadows to see you through.[11]

My friend June Hunt has a special gift for sharing appropriate Scripture in difficult times. During one of my darkest hours, she reminded me of Isaiah's words: "When you pass *through* the waters, I will be with you; and *through* the rivers, they shall not overflow you. When you walk *through* the fire, you shall not be burned, nor shall the flame scorch you."[12] June highlighted the key thought in Isaiah's comforting prophecy of encouragement—i.e., the word *through*. You are never left without His hand, and ultimately you will always make your way *through* the difficulties. The Lord has brought me *through* again and again. God has been and will always be faithful to me and to you![13]

You can live in a dark and hurting world because you have the light of Christ within. The blessedness after death will come as an extension of the blessedness here on earth, the harvest of what has been sown on earth. This blessedness is not something to be sought from God or given by God at your request; rather, it is the result and fulfillment of your obedience to certain conditions that the Lord has set before you.

Blessings or Blessedness?

The blessings (Greek *eulogeō*, lit. "to speak well of" or in transliteration the English word "eulogize") that you ask from the Lord in prayer have nothing to do with this blessedness (Greek *makarios*, lit.

"happy") about which the Lord is speaking in the Sermon on the Mount. Your asking for the blessings of God should presuppose a realization of your own sinfulness and emptiness. Such a request from your heart should be your way of asking God to fill that emptiness through His favor and grace.

When God speaks or "says a good word," His energy is released and His power is made known.[14] In a sense when you ask for His blessing, you are asking Him to personalize His blessings by making His promises applicable to you individually.[15] You are pleading for His mercy and grace, asking Him to speak a good word for you, even though you do not deserve it.

The request for God's blessing refers then to God's activity in your life. You are asking Him to do something in your life.[16] You should be willing to accept His will for your life rather than expecting Him to acquiesce to your plans. You can also "bless" God in the sense of "speaking well" or eulogizing Him as you offer praise and thanksgiving to Him.[17]

On the other hand, the blessedness described in the Beatitudes is not a quality characteristic of human beings but a trait of God Himself. Only God imparts this blessedness, and no human being can "bless" God in this sense. This blessedness cannot be demanded from God but rather is the result of fulfilling the prescribed conditions set before you by the Lord Himself. Blessedness is a characteristic exclusively bestowed by God upon the believer, and it is attainable by you only because God dwells in your heart.

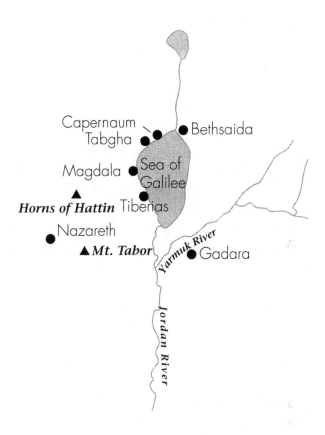

The Sermon on the Mount was probably preached somewhere near the Sea of Galilee. Though Jerome and others have identified the spot as Mount Tabor, the natural amphitheater that lies between Tell Hum and et-Tabgha, called the Horns of Hattin, seems more compatible with both Matthew's description of a "mountain" (Matt. 5:1) and Luke's reference to a "level place" (Luke 6:17).

Moments for Enrichment

1. A careful reading of the context of Matthew 5–7, and especially of the immediate context of Matthew 5:1–12, will help to put the focal passage in perspective.

2. Your consideration of the word study on "blessed" here in the introduction as well as in the first chapter of this book will lay the foundation for the meaning of this word as it is used in Scripture and especially in the Sermon on the Mount.

3. A personal worksheet can be fashioned from the chart "My BeAttitudes for Spiritual Growth" on page 14.

4. A study of the map of Israel on page 11, will give you a look at the region of Galilee and help you visualize possible settings for the sermon.

The Focal Text

And seeing the multitudes, He went up on a mountain, and when He was seated His disciples came to Him.

Then He opened His mouth and taught them, saying:
"Blessed are the poor in spirit,
For theirs is the kingdom of heaven.
Blessed are those who mourn,
For they shall be comforted.
Blessed are the meek,
For they shall inherit the earth.
Blessed are those who hunger and thirst for righteousness,
For they shall be filled.
Blessed are the merciful,
For they shall obtain mercy.
Blessed are the pure in heart,
For they shall see God.
Blessed are the peacemakers,
For they shall be called sons of God.
Blessed are those who are persecuted for righteousness' sake,
For theirs is the kingdom of heaven.
Blessed are you when they revile and persecute you, and say
all kinds of evil against you falsely for My sake.
Rejoice and be exceedingly glad, for great is your reward in
heaven, for so they persecuted the prophets who were
before you."
Matthew 5:1–12

See also Luke 6:20–23 for a parallel passage.

My BeAttitudes for Spiritual Growth

BeAttitude Goal	Bible Reference	Steps to Reach Goal	Entry Date	Date Realized

Notes

1. Rom. 12:2.
2. 2 Cor. 12:9.
3. 2 Cor. 5:17.
4. Philip Yancey, "Be Ye Perfect, More or Less," *Christianity Today* (17 July 1995, 38–41.
5. See also Luke 6:20–49.
6. See a description of this "new commandment" in John 13:34; 1 John 2:8; 2 John 5.
7. Ps. 119:105.
8. Rom. 12:1–2.
9. Gal. 2:20.
10. 1 Cor. 2:7–16; see also Luke 12:15.
11. Deut. 31:6.
12. Isa. 43:2 (italics added).
13. Lam. 3:22–23.
14. Luke 1:28.
15. Luke 11:28.
16. Rom. 4:8.
17. Eph. 1:3.

⹕ 1 ⹕

Wealth in Search of Poverty

BE HUMBLE:
LET YOUR ATTITUDE BE MARKED WITH HUMILITY

The Context: Matthew 5:3–12

"Blessed are the poor in spirit,
For theirs is the kingdom of heaven."

MATTHEW 5:3

Being humble or "poor in spirit" does not require poverty of possessions. Ruth Hunt depended upon the Lord as have few other women I have known. As the widow of H. L. Hunt, who during his lifetime was considered to be the richest and most powerful man in the world, Ruth certainly had an abundance of worldly possessions—priceless art, valuable antique furnishings, a spacious and picturesque estate. And she generously undergirded countless ministries through her inspiring stewardship and generous philanthropic giving. She was a most gracious hostess and opened her home regularly to friends and neighbors as well as to acquaintances and strangers.

But all that she gave and did for others is not what most endeared Ruth to me and to many others; rather, it was the humility she expressed when she went to the Lord to present her own spiritual needs. Ruth Hunt and I have wept together and prayed together. When I visited her on the bed of affliction, she never failed to pray for me. I always felt that she loved me and enjoyed my fellowship—whether as the young wife of the president of an insignificant struggling Bible institute or as the wife of the respected president of one of the largest seminaries in the world. I shared simple joys and sorrows with her and she with me. Ruth Hunt, in her humility, exemplified the godly trait of being "poor in spirit."

In the Beatitudes, the character traits of a Christian are first described in general terms,[1] and then they are measured by the world's reaction to those traits.[2] The description is both negative and positive. It includes certain things that happen to an individual *because* she is that kind of Christian. Every one of these statements contradicts the existing standards of the world. On first glance the principles seem mild and negative; but in actuality they are revolutionary and positive. As such, they are the only hope for the world then or now.

A Woman's Wisdom

"Being a Christian is not doing certain things but doing everything a certain way."

—Mary Crowley

The first beatitude is the foundation on which all Christian character must be built, and the last beatitude describes the relationship of such Christian character to the environment in which it is found. Both the first and last beatitudes describe results that are already possessed, while the others speak of results that are to come in the future.

What Does It Mean to Be "Blessed"?

The common denominator and most important word in each beatitude is "blessed" (Greek *makarios*). In early Greek poetry, a form of "blessed" was used to describe the deities, who were supposed to be in contrast with mere mortals. The Greeks believed that the gods were "blessed" in themselves, unaffected by the outside world with its poverty and death. Later the term came to be used of people, especially of the dead who had been liberated from the influences of the outside world. Though in early Greek usage the word was used largely to indicate outward prosperity, in this context the word will not lend itself to such interpretation since the very opposite is apparent. In fact, the meaning of this word has been transformed through its usage in the New Testament.

The word occurs eight times in Matthew 5:3–10. No verb accompanies the word in the Greek text. Originally, "blessed" (Greek *makarios*) referred to a state that is neither caused nor affected by outside circumstances. The word expressed an attitude that issues forth as a result of what is within. Even the acquisition of worldly goods cannot ultimately determine the measure of happiness or blessedness in a person's life.

A popular woman speaker announced to a large group of eager listeners, "*You* are the key to your happiness!" The truth of the matter is that the key to happiness is far beyond the resources of any woman, but every woman, including those in that auditorium, *chooses* how to use the "key to happiness" that is available to all through the sovereign work of the Holy Spirit. Only the woman within whom God lives and dwells is "blessed" in the sense that her outer circumstances cannot destroy or overwhelm the inner resources God has given. This blessing does not come from the woman herself and her devices, but rather it comes from beyond self or anything the world has to offer. This blessing comes from God Himself, whose intrinsic blessedness is woven into the warp and woof of His Being.

Blessedness more than anything else is spiritual fruit. God Himself is the key ingredient.[3] He is better, sweeter, and more abundant than anything the world has to offer, and He is eternal—without beginning or ending.[4]

Such a prescription for blessedness cannot be appropriated until you have committed your life to Christ. The commandment is not that you are *to be blessed* but rather that you are *to fulfill the conditions that open you to receive the blessed state.* That degree of blessedness is determined by your fulfilling the conditions set forth by the Lord in the Sermon on the Mount. To fulfill only one condition would provide you with only a fraction of the blessedness God makes available.

The term *blessed,* sometimes paraphrased as *happy,* is regarded by some as rather pious—even presumptuous—holiness. Unfortunately, the current meaning of *happy* in the English language has taken on a rather frivolous connotation that is far from what is meant by the Greek term *makarios,* a word that contained the idea of a stable, adjusted, secure person. The reference is to an indestructible joy that is not uprooted by suffering, sorrow, or even your own demise. The emphasis is upon *character within* and not *circumstances without* because its point of reference is in the person of the perfect Lord and not in mundane human frailties.

Nothing from without can take from within you the presence of the Lord. The Lord lifted this concept to the highest plane of human life through His embodiment of the principles of which He spoke. Herodotus, the Greek historian[5] used this same word to describe an oasis in the African desert, setting the pattern for its later meaning in Scripture.

The ancient Greeks also described the island of Cyprus as *makarios* or "Cyprus, the blessed one." They were acknowledging that this beautiful, well-watered, and fertile island provided all the sustenance and happiness needed so that its inhabitants would never have to go beyond its coastline. The island was famous for its fruits and flowers. Strabo[6] recorded that the island produced abundant oil, corn, and wine. The elder Pliny[7] referred to the many minerals and precious stones, including the diamond, that were found on this strategic island. The island's extensive forests supplied timber for shipbuilding.

The parallel is obvious: For the Christian, the Lord has within Himself everything that will bring genuine happiness. The rich resources of the beautiful island of Cyprus are in no way comparable to the riches found in Christ Jesus.[8]

By simply receiving Jesus Christ as personal Savior, you enter His family, receiving for yourself the nature and character of His son, together with the natural inheritance of the blessedness He bestows on His own. You cannot have what God has without having God Himself. On the other hand, you can be poor, hungry, persecuted, and distressed in every way and still be blessed just because you have the living L   dwelling in your heart.

The Christian woman can have within herself all she needs to be happy so that her happiness is not dependent upon personal good fortune but rather upon the divine resources residing within her own heart because of her personal relationship with Jesus Christ. Jesus refuted the notion that blessedness or happiness is in any way tied to personal prosperity. He clearly directed His words to the realm of the personal and inner character of the individual rather than the public and outer perceptions of others. You might say that this happiness is possessed by a woman here and now on this earth as well as there and then in heaven because of who she is now as well as what she shall be then.[9]

In Psalm 1, the psalmist compared blessedness to a stately and secure "tree planted by rivers of water." The usage of the word *blessed* in the Old Testament is consistent in implying that the standard for happiness is based on moral qualities rather than human circumstances. This parallel is especially apparent in the Septuagint (a Greek translation of the Old Testament), which continues to use the same Greek words found in the Matthew account (see the Beatitudes in the Psalms chart on page 43 and the Old Testament Beatitudes chart on pages 41–42).

How Can You Be Blessed?

Your attitude is the prevailing influence in determining your responses, and your attitude will be determined by the way you look at a situation rather than by the situation itself.

A Humorous Anecdote

Consider this amusing couplet illustrating the contradiction created by a difference in perspective:

Two men looked out from prison bars.
One saw mud; the other saw stars.

Jesus does not ignore a woman's desire for inner joy, peace, and harmony. He knows that all of these are essential to a meaningful life. But He also knows that in the midst of the joys will be circumstances difficult to endure and days through which it is hard to walk. Happiness to the heart can be compared to bright sunshine in the landscape, to vibrant color in the artist's palette, to pungent spices in gourmet cuisine, to picturesque figures of speech in a literary master-piece, and to melodious music in the symphony hall.

Above all, Jesus taught that happiness—this coveted good—is not found by *seeking* but by *doing,* and not only in *doing* but even more in *being.* The state of blessedness is much more profound than the condition of happiness as the latter term is generally used in contem-porary society.

The Prelude of Spiritual Helplessness

The wise people of the world have always despised anyone who was "poor in spirit," anyone whom they considered to be a weakling or wimp. Anyone lacking in courage was viewed as a sorry excuse for a man or a woman. Someone with self-confidence and a take-charge atti-tude has usually been the one sought, admired, and followed in every realm of life.

On the other hand, the Christian woman is blessed *because* she realizes her own spiritual helplessness. Poverty of spirit is essential for all Christian growth and development of character. It describes your attitude toward God, self, and the world. This poverty of spirit was never meant to be an end in itself. Rather, it is a means to move you toward the end result. In fact, there is no entry into the kingdom without this fundamental quality since it means an empty-ing. A woman cannot be filled with the Spirit until she has been emptied of self.

Many conferences promote the "higher life," but few call for the "lowly life." Accordingly, much is heard about being "filled with the

Spirit," but little is said about the necessity of first "emptying yourself" to make room for the Spirit! You are continually reminded of personal worth and significance but seldom told that laying hold of Christ presupposes letting go of yourself and recognizing your own inherent worthlessness until your heart is emptied of self and filled with Him.[10]

A Woman's Wisdom

"All the spiritual writers of past generations have recognised (sic) this joy in God, and all of them have written concerning the stripping process that seems necessary to bring us to it. They have called this process by different names, some calling it 'inward desolation,' and some the 'winter of the soul,' . . . but all meaning one and the same thing; and that thing is the experience of finding all earthly joys stained or taken away, in order to drive the soul to God alone."

—Hannah Whitall Smith

The word *poor* (Greek *ptochoi*) is derived from a root meaning "crouch," which would suggest a beggar who kneels at the feet of others in hopes that they would supply her needs. Those in helplessness and desperate need are driven to a dependent relationship with God, who alone can supply these needs or provide the ability to bear up under the burden.

The connotation is of one who is poor but does not satisfy her own needs, one who is dependent upon another to whom she is answerable. She is dependent upon the alms or resources of other people. The help and rescue of this destitute beggar must come from the outside. Such need and destitution in a spiritual sense comes only when a woman has so committed her life to Christ that self has been put to death.[11] Then she is powerless in her own strength and willing to rely upon the Lord to meet her needs.

Mary Crowley, a Dallas businesswoman who founded and built a multimillion-dollar company based upon biblical principles, consistently exercised her stewardship by giving generously to kingdom causes. Around her neck she wore a gold chain with an unusual enhancer: two golden shovels—one large and one small. The larger one represented what God was doing, and the smaller one pictured her own efforts. No one can outgive God or even equal His generous outpouring. God always has the bigger shovel!

When any woman is stripped of her pride, she is able to be responsive to God's Word through His person and in the midst of His gracious ministries in her behalf. All self-sufficiency is put aside, and she is able to revel in the blessedness of knowing that the Lord is all-sufficient.

The Example of Servanthood

The Lord also demonstrated this poverty of spirit as the Suffering Servant in Isaiah, "As a sheep before its shearers is silent, So He opened not His mouth."[12] Even in His silence, the Lord expressed His humble spirit with eloquence.

The account of Jesus' testing in the wilderness is found in Matthew 4:1–11. Satan tried to get Jesus to abandon the "poverty of spirit" so perfectly exemplified in His life. Satan asked Jesus again and again to grasp and to maintain His rights and to demonstrate His Sonship to God in the world's way by making stones into bread[13] (an appeal to the physical appetite); by throwing Himself down from the top of the temple's pinnacle[14] (a call for spectacular display in pride); or by seizing control of earthly kingdoms[15] (an effort to awaken in Him an ambition for power). All these temptations were directed toward trying to get Jesus to abandon His "poverty of spirit." Yet through all Jesus modeled extraordinary humility; and by incorporating this principle into His own life, He taught His disciples to possess the same spirit. His defense against the Tempter came from Scripture.[16] He refused to compromise, choosing instead to follow the humble path of selflessness, servanthood, and suffering.

Jesus made clear that *entry* into the kingdom was conditioned on the very same principle—i.e., being "poor in spirit"—that predicated *growth* in the kingdom. You begin the Christian life where the Savior began—"In my hand no price I bring, Simply to thy cross I cling."[17] Jesus knows that if you become what He wants you to be, you will do the right thing. If you are "poor in spirit," you will also be true to your responsibilities to your fellow pilgrims. Each beatitude is a paradox, and this is no exception.

As with most godly traits, the pattern is found in the life of Jesus, who humbled Himself in order to make atonement for our sins on the cross.[18] From His humble birth in a crude stable in the insignificant village of Bethlehem, He went against culture in following a path of servanthood to reach His exaltation. His followers were called to deny themselves in order to offer themselves in service to others, even to put their lives on the line.[19] The only praise for humility comes from God. It is not something to add to your resume!

The verb in this verse is not in the future tense, which puts the believer in possession of great wealth, even as at the same time she is already in possession of great poverty. An interesting example of this occurs in the life of the Lord through use of the phrase, "Son of man." The first time, the Son of Man "has nowhere to lay His head";[20] the last time, the Son of Man has "on His head a golden crown."[21] What a beautiful outworking of this principle is illustrated in the life of the Lord Himself! Through the Beatitudes the Lord declares His personhood and His work. His life was characterized primarily by two things: humility and sacrifice. In order to be like Him, your life, too, must be marked by humility and sacrifice, and these are not natural goals. Submission is difficult partially because it, too, demands humility and service.

You may be tempted to think that the only woman who is genuinely "poor in spirit" is one who makes a great sacrifice or one who withdraws from life and its responsibilities. However, poverty in itself is nowhere affirmed as the path to blessedness. In fact, poverty may lead to spiritual pride on one hand or to bitterness and hostility on the other.

In the Old Testament, humility often indicates lowliness or even affliction.[22] In the New Testament, another nuance of meaning develops as the word suggests a demeanor that assumes dependence upon God and respect for others. Certainly this character quality is a spiritual discipline that results in a holy and set-apart lifestyle and not a character trait that naturally evolves from human instinct.

Some religious monasteries have been luxurious and those who inhabited them indulgent. For example, the French painter Victor Marias-Milton[23] enjoyed painting scenes from the lives of Catholic cardinals. He delighted in colorful compositions of their luxurious living, such as the oil painting entitled "A Tasty Bite." In this painting the cardinal, who has devoted his life to serving God, is sitting at a table draped with elegant linens trimmed in lace and savoring a beautifully garnished lobster accompanied by a glass of wine, and he is surrounded by tapestries and antique furnishings.

On the other hand, Siddhartha Gautama (who became known as Buddha)[24] abandoned his position and wealth and refused all association with the comforts of life. At one point in his life, Siddhartha was very cynical and taught that the desires of life were evil and that the only salvation for the human spirit was to escape from this life. Nevertheless, he later came to see that ascetic practices in and of themselves do not lead to spiritual power.[25]

From the perspective of many, it is easy to understand the sinfulness of self-indulgence as depicted by the French painter's scene. However, it is not so easy to see the danger of the self-deprivation projected by men like Siddhartha. Yet even a commitment to self-deprivation and isolation is meaningless in itself. Merely to make a great sacrifice or to retire from a life of pleasure or to put aside earthly responsibilities is not a sure path to heavenly reward.

The Lord chose familiar terms to describe His principles of character, but the revolutionary concepts embodied in those terms are apparent. His reference to the "poor" implied not necessarily or even primarily those who lacked worldly goods. The "poor" of whom Jesus spoke were the godly. The afflicted, the lowly, and the humble-minded are in contrast to those who are self-satisfied, arrogant, and proud.

A Woman's Wisdom

"The fire of God's love must burn up self-love and self-will and let the soul appear, beautiful and full of grace, as it was meant to be when God created us."

—Catherine of Siena

Genuine humility is the badge of greatness. It is ultimately an attitude a woman assumes toward herself.[26] This attitude is in contrast to the world's view, which encourages every woman to believe in herself, express herself, and grasp position and rights for herself.

God's way is in direct contrast. He urges us to deny ourselves, to lose our lives,[27] and to give preference to others.[28] Consider Mary, the mother of the Lord, who even after being informed of her great honor in becoming the mother of Messiah, submitted herself in obedience to the Father and lifted her voice in praise to Him.[29]

A Woman's Wisdom

"There are two ways of spreading light: to be the candle or the mirror that reflects it."

—Edith Wharton

Mary of Nazareth lived her life in obedience to her parents and also in personal holiness and purity according to the words of the Lord. Her response to the angel Gabriel's announcement was a harbinger to her keen understanding of Scripture and her readiness to obey God whatever the cost.[30] Her heart was set toward making a home for Joseph to whom she was betrothed, and toward rearing the children her heart desired. Certainly Mary's parents must have been proud of her, and they must have rejoiced in the wise choices Mary had made throughout her childhood and adolescence. They must have also been pleased with the contract they had established for her marriage to a man of Joseph's stature. Even Mary herself must have felt a sense of personal achievement as she moved closer to her goals.

Then God intervened in Mary's life, not by giving her all the desires of her heart but by challenging the roots of her faith and putting all her personal dreams and plans in jeopardy. Suddenly she became an outcast woman who was perceived by others as living in sin and shame. The pride her parents had felt for their beautiful and dutiful daughter, the satisfaction that had filled Mary's own soul—all these were stripped away. Humility took on a new dimension in her life as she realized more and more that, in her own strength, she could do nothing to alleviate her pain or escape the seeming injustice dealt her.

When my husband and I left the seminary with our Th.M.s in hand and his Th.D. almost complete, we felt a sense of accomplishment and pride that we had weathered financial pressures, debilitating illness, some injustice in professorial grading because of our theological positions, and the pressures of a fussy church. We left seminary to go to a prestigious and coveted pastorate in an academic community. Of course, I expected to be asked to teach the Bible to women because of my theological preparation and experience. But that did not happen. In fact, most of the teaching of women I did in that community was at the public library!

I worked with different groups in the church and threw myself into the ministries of the church, but the church already had a female Bible teacher who studied and prepared and expected to teach. She did not seem too excited over my presence—at least not in the arena of teaching the Bible to women. Stripped of my expectations, I found myself entering my own "wilderness" of preparation. As my preschoolers napped, I began with Genesis and read to Revelation again and again, asking myself with each reading, "What is God saying to me as a woman? Who am I? What am I to do in the kingdom? Will I ever use the theological preparation I have worked so hard to complete?"

And out of that "wilderness" experience was born a series of messages—The Bible Speaks on Being a Woman—that formed the underpinnings of my ministries to women through the years. Stripped of pride in light of the tools I had acquired—Greek, Hebrew, theological foundations, effective ways of communicating a message—and without accolades for the high academic standing I had attained, I humbled myself before the Lord. He sent me to the "wilderness" to learn to wait on Him.

Only in being humble before the Lord do you learn the place for solitude; only in quietness do you develop the discipline for a time of communication with Him as separate and distinct from preparing for a particular assignment in ministry. The line is drawn between self-confident pride to rest on what you have already done and the God-confident boldness to forge ahead to an uncertain future.

Humility is a quality dear to the heart of Christ.[31] It serves to hallow all life's experiences. Humility becomes the basis for blessedness and puts a premium on personality or character *within* rather than on possessions or circumstances *without.* Through humility you are released from the grip of that which is temporal and of the world in order to realize the value of the eternal.

In my own life, I find just as much pleasure in managing my routine household tasks as in my public responsibilities of teaching and speaking. As the "first lady" on the seminary campus, I preside as hostess over many elegant functions; but I must still take delight in more mundane tasks like carrying around the trash bag to clean up after the international students' luncheon. At this time I can speak to each student individually and offer service to some who are continually serving others.

A Woman's Wisdom

"Humility is an 'invisible grace'—those who possess it are unaware of it."

—Penelope J. Stokes

To be "poor in spirit" is the most fundamental characteristic of the Christian because there is no way to enter the kingdom of God apart from this poverty of spirit. Humility demands an emptying, while the other principles show a fullness. Logic would dictate that you cannot be filled until you are first empty. Conviction must precede conversion. In the gospel there is condemnation before conversion and reconciliation. The Sermon on the Mount puts before every believer a mountain to scale with an awesome height to attain. There is no hope of climbing that mountain until you first realize that you cannot ascend on your own power and in your own strength.

I've had only one experience in mountain climbing. When I was in my mid-thirties, my son Armour and I had the opportunity to climb the mountain traditionally identified as Sinai (or Mt. Horeb) located in Egypt. We began the ascent about 3:30 A.M. and did not complete our descent until late afternoon. I distinctly remember the arduous physical challenges to me—a woman not known for athletic prowess or physical exercise.

What I remember most was the tender care and tenacious determination of my son that I *would* complete the task! He went up and down that mountain countless times as he forged ahead in his enthusiasm but then in compassion backtracked to encourage and even physically pull me onward to the summit. In no way could I have made it to the top of that mountain if a young boy who loved me and believed in me and *helped* me had not been at my side!

This personal anecdote from my own life serves as a reminder that the spiritual mountains of life can only be conquered with the Holy Spirit, moving alongside to encourage and pull you along in the way of the Lord.[32]

The Challenge of Selfless Reliance

The world says that to get ahead and achieve what is important you must believe in yourself and express yourself and realize your potential. Such self-confidence and self-reliance promise you a place of your own in the world. On the other hand, God's way is for you to come face-to-face with Him. In so doing, you are reduced, by His very presence, to being "poor of spirit."

Such humility means a complete absence of pride, a void of self-assurance, the abandonment of self-reliance. It means a consciousness that you are nothing in the presence of an awesome God. There must be an overwhelming awareness of your utter nothingness and helplessness when you come face-to-face with God. Any natural position in life, any bestowed powers, and any achieved morality are to be put aside because they in themselves are worthless.

Consider this Grammatical Note

Only beatitude one and beatitude eight, which refer to the kingdom of heaven as the promise, use the present tense. When a beatitude promises something other than the kingdom, that promise is in the future tense. Certainly the Lord does not intimate that those who accept Him as Savior will have all their blessings relegated to the distant future. On the contrary, there are blessings for you here and now. Though the ultimate fulfillment awaits the future, God dwells in believers right now. He lives and works among His people even now.

You do not become "poor in spirit" by looking at yourself or by devising any plans of your own. Rather, you must look only at God. Read His book;[33] study His words;[34] consider the principles found in Scripture;[35] meditate upon His life.[36] You cannot do this or look at Him in this way without feeling in yourself absolute poverty of spirit and placing complete hope in Him.

> Yea, all I need, in Thee to find,
> O Lamb of God, I come.[37]

Of course, no one would ever say that the Christian is *self-sufficient,* but you can say that a woman with Jesus Christ in her heart becomes *God-sufficient.* In other words, the Christian woman is not concerned about her *self-image* but rather about the *God-image* in her life. She must focus on being God-sufficient and not circumstance-conditioned, which puts the emphasis where it ought to be—on God's power rather than on human resourcefulness.

A Woman's Wisdom

"God can make you anything you want to be, but you have to put everything in his hands."

—Mahalia Jackson

The Paradox of Helpful Helplessness

God chose the state of poverty as that in which He could most effectively do His work. Jesus could have been born into wealth and power, for certainly He is the creator and ruler of the universe. However, God chose to send His Son into poverty.[38] A spiritual parallel is found: In poverty there is the absence of much that seems to hinder the acceptance of the gospel, i.e., self-sufficiency, pride, and the absence of need. Poverty, then, is a condition that enables believers to accept blessedness more readily because they are already at the end of their own resources.

This blessedness overshadows uneasiness and want and rejects dissatisfaction and complaint. Upon receiving Christ as Savior, a woman receives the living Lord to dwell within her heart, thereby acquiring access to His character, which in itself is sufficient so that she is not dependent upon external circumstances for satisfaction. She moves from self-sufficiency and fleshly concerns to God sufficiency and spiritual joy.

Naomi did not always respond to her afflictions appropriately. She left Bethlehem with her family because of a famine—an empty cupboard. She returned from pagan Moab, leaving a full cupboard but bereft of husband and sons. She had learned the meaning of emptiness. However, even in the midst of her affliction and emptiness, God had given her Ruth, a devoted daughter-in-law.[39]

Just as any woman following her natural instincts would do, Naomi blamed God for her misfortune. She forgot about the fact that affliction is a necessary factor in spiritual growth. She called the Lord "Shaddai" (Hebrew, meaning literally "all-sufficiency"), and yet through her questioning His dealings with her she refused to accept the sufficiency He offered.[40] Naomi needed to be reminded as do many women, that God must be trusted for "better or worse" and that He is at His best when you are at your worst. When you are overcome with weakness, His strength comes into play to sustain and encourage.[41]

A Woman's Wisdom

Don't let controversy hurt your soul. Live near to God by prayer. Just fall down at his feet and open your very soul before him, and throw yourself right into his arms.

Some women assume that to be "poor in spirit" demands a certain outer look. They want to dismiss any attention to the outer frame with no makeup and the absence of color and style in dress. This concept is not the sense of the passage since one certainly is not admonished in any way to draw attention to herself or to package herself outwardly into any mold. In fact, the sense of Scripture is just the opposite.

Ruth the Moabitess prepared herself to go down to the threshing floor to make an appeal to Boaz, her goel/redeemer. She washed and perfumed her body and adorned herself in her most flattering garment.[42] Queen Esther also put aside her sackcloth of mourning and dressed in her royal robes to appear before Ahasuerus to plead for her people.[43] In both cases, these women humbled themselves to make a serious entreaty. Each exemplified "poverty of spirit," and yet each wanted to look her best for such an awesome task. The "woman of strength" in Proverbs clothed herself in elegance as she went about her daily tasks. Yet without question, the "fear of the Lord" she had within her heart marked her life with a winsome humility that endeared her to all who knew her.[44]

After all, the outer frame draws others to your testimony within.[45] In the same way, if clothing or jewelry or styling of hair or painting of face becomes the focus in itself so that attention is drawn only to a part of the outer frame, then a woman has failed just as tragically in her task of magnifying the Lord.[46] Nothing on the outside should glitter so brightly that it blinds onlookers to the beauty of the Christ within. Your goal should always be that the world in looking at you will crave to know the cause of your joy within and be open to the Lord Jesus Christ.[47]

The woman who is conscious of spiritual poverty is aware of her limitations. She does not have the character of the Pharisee, who did not feel any spiritual need. Rather, she identifies with the publican, who felt his spiritual poverty and confessed himself to be a sinner.[48] She not only recognizes her own spiritual shortcomings, but she also desires to be better and realizes that in herself she has nothing with which to meet that need. This condition alone is necessary to enter the kingdom, and it is within the reach of everyone who is willing to accept God's grace as a free gift.

The woman who is "poor in spirit" is blessed because she has the kingdom of God as a natural sequence and not as an arbitrary reward. This blessedness or happiness is not created by new surroundings, but new surroundings are created by happiness. A woman is happy and blessed because of her character, and she then changes her environment because she herself has been changed. The woman who stands outside certain circumstances of life, saying, "Oh, if only I were in those circumstances, I would be happy," would not be a candidate for this genuine happiness. Again, the flaw in this argument is that happiness is not rooted in outward circumstances but in an inward condition of character.

Certainly there is always the dimension of the "poor in spirit" as being dependent upon God for help and vindication (see Isa. 61:1, in which the Hebrew term 'nwm was applied specifically to God's people who remained faithful to Him and His law despite their affliction in exile). The "poor in spirit" are the desperate—those who stand before God without pretense, stripped of self-sufficiency, self-security, and self-righteousness.

Remember the Syro-Phoenician woman who did not receive her desperate petition until she became poor in spirit. This pagan woman made her request irresistible to God when she acknowledged Jesus as the rightful king,[49] accepted Him as her king,[50] and then humbly asked for His help.[51] She realized her own helplessness and would not turn from seeking the Lord and relying upon Him.

The kingdom of heaven is peerless and endless, excelling all other kingdoms. It is God's place for expressing His initiative in history through Jesus Christ to redeem you to a proper relationship with Himself. God unveils His desire to stand at the center of your life and to enable you to be reconciled to Himself. "The hope of a kingdom . . . should carry a Christian with courage and cheerfulness through all his afflictions."[52]

The New Testament has three uses of the phrase "kingdom of heaven," all of which could be applied to this verse: (1) the kingdom of God within the heart of a believer,[53] (2) the body made up of all Christians on earth,[54] and (3) the kingdom prepared for believers after death.[55] Yet in each case it is God who ushers in the kingdom, and Jesus is the reigning king.

Any who turn without pretense to God through the person and ministry of Jesus Christ are "blessed." This entry to the kingdom is clearly by grace, not works. Only those who are "poor in spirit" and thus have no personal merit to offer can enter. This acknowledgment of spiritual poverty prepares the human heart for God's gift of salvation. To become "poor in spirit," look at God! Make Christ the end and motivation for all you do! Remember that for you as a woman, humility should be like underwear—you can't leave home without it, but you don't want it showing!

Prayer and Meditation

"Father, whate'er of earthly bliss thy sov'reign will denies,
Accepted at thy throne of grace, let this petition rise.
Give me a calm, a thankful heart, from every murmur
*   free;*
The blessings of thy grace impart, and let me live to thee.
Let the sweet hope that thou art mine my path of life
*   attend;*
Thy presence thro' my journey shine, and crown my
*   journey's end."*

—Anne Steele

Moments for Enrichment

A VERSE TO MEMORIZE

"Humble yourselves in the sight of the Lord, and He will lift you up" (James 4:10).

ACTIVITIES TO ENHANCE YOUR UNDERSTANDING OF THE TEXT

1. Concordance entries for "blessed" will help you get an overview of how the word is used elsewhere in Scripture. Additional translations of the text may add nuances of meaning that are helpful.

2. Charts that track the usage of "blessed" through the rest of Scripture are included. You can expand these and add your own insights by describing the character qualities noted and those you will add (see Old Testament Beatitudes chart on pages 41–42 and the Beatitudes in the Psalms chart on page 43). Use the Beatitudes for Women chart on page 48 as a guide for developing these charts.

3. In writing your own definition of happiness, list specific things or circumstances that would contribute to your personal happiness. Then you are ready to note ways you can *be* and things you can *do* to find genuine happiness.

4. A time for prayerful introspection may produce some positive steps you can take toward stripping away self-centered characteristics and becoming "poor in spirit."

Self-Centered Characteristic in My Life	Way to Remove this Trait from My Life
Pride	
Self-sufficiency	

5. Complete the contrast between the kingdom of this world and the
   kingdom of Christ.

The Kingdom of this World Equals	The Kingdom of Christ Equals	Biblical Reference
Great Possessions		
Accumulated Wealth		
Increased Power		

6. List some specific ways you can develop an attitude of humility.

My Goal	Ways to Attain the Goal	Challenge from Scripture

Old Testament Beatitudes

Beatitude	Character Quality	Description	Reference
"For *blessed* are those who keep my ways."	Faithful		Proverbs 8:32
"*Blessed* is the man who listens to me, watching daily at my gates, waiting at the posts of my doors."	Attentive		Proverbs 8:34
"The righteous man walks in his integrity; his children are *blessed* after him."	Honest		Proverbs 20:7
"He who has a generous eye will be *blessed*, for he gives of his bread to the poor."	Generous		Proverbs 22:9
"*Blessed* are all those who wait for Him."	Patient		Isaiah 30:18
"*Blessed* are you who sow beside all waters, who send out freely the feet of the ox and the donkey."	Resourceful		Isaiah 32:20
"*Blessed* is the man who does this . . . who keeps from defiling the Sabbath. And keeps his hand from doing any evil."	Righteous		Isaiah 56:2

Old Testament Beatitudes

Beatitude	Character Quality	Description	Reference
"*Blessed* is the man who trusts in the LORD, and whose hope is in the LORD."	Committed		Jeremiah 17:7
"*Blessed* is he who waits."	Steadfast		Daniel 12:12

NOTE: The word *blessed* (Heb. *'esher* is literally "being straight" or "being level, right," and by implication "going forward," "being honest," "prospering," and "being happy."

Beatitudes in the Psalms

Beatitude	Character Quality	Description	Reference
"Blessed is the man who walks not in the counsel of the ungodly, nor stands in the path of sinners, nor sits in the seat of the scornful."	Righteousness		Psalm 1:1
"Blessed are all those who put their trust in Him."	Trusting Faith		Psalm 2:12

Other New Testament Beatitudes

Beatitude	Character Quality	Description	Reference
"And *blessed* is he who is not offended because of Me."	Bold		Matthew 11:6
"But *blessed* are your eyes for they see, and your ears for they hear."	Sensitive		Matthew 13:16
"*Blessed* is she who believed, for there will be a fulfillment of those things which were told her from the Lord."	Trusting		Luke 1:45
"*Blessed* are the eyes which see the things you see."	Available		Luke 10:23
"*Blessed* is the womb that bore You, and the breasts which nursed You!"	Anointed		Luke 11:27
"More than that, *blessed* are those who hear the word of God and keep it!"	Obedient		Luke 11:28
"*Blessed* are those servants whom the master, when he comes, will find watching."	Watchful		Luke 12:37

Other New Testament Beatitudes

Beatitude	Character Quality	Description	Reference
"Blessed is that servant whom his master will find so doing when he comes."	Faithful		Luke 12:43
"Blessed is he who shall eat bread in the kingdom of God!"	Obedient		Luke 14:15
"Blessed are those who have not seen and yet have believed."	Possessing Faith		John 20:29
"Blessed are those whose lawless deeds are forgiven, and whose sins are covered; *Blessed* is the man to whom the LORD shall not impute sin."	Redeemed		Romans 4:7–8
"Blessed is the man who endures temptation; for when he has been approved, he will receive the crown of life, which the Lord has promised to those who love him."	Steadfast		James 1:12

Other New Testament Beatitudes

Beatitude	Character Quality	Description	Reference
"But he who looks into the perfect law of liberty and continues in it, and is not a forgetful hearer but a doer of the word, this one will be *blessed* in what he does."	Consistent		James 1:25

NOTE: *"Blessed"* (Greek *makarios*) suggests that you are supremely "blest," "fortunate," and "well off."

Old Testament Beatitudes in the Book of Revelation

Beatitude	Emphasis	Reference
1. The blessedness of those reading, hearing, and keeping this prophecy.	1. The importance of the Word of God.	Revelation 1:3
2. The happiness of the dead who die in the Lord.	2. The blessings of eternal life.	Revelation 14:13
3. The respect of those watching and keeping their garments.	3. The anticipation of the Lord's return.	Revelation 16:15
4. The delight of those invited to the marriage supper of the Lamb.	4. The joy of God's presence.	Revelation 19:9
5. The blessedness of those who participate in the first resurrection.	5. The freedom of deliverance from death.	Revelation 20:6
6. The joy of keeping the words of this prophecy.	6. The necessity of obedience to the Word.	Revelation 22:7
7. The happy result of washing one's robe and accessing the Tree of Life.	7. The guarantee of eternal sustenance.	Revelation 22:14

Beatitudes for Women

Blessed are . . .	Character Quality	Description	References
those who are poor in spirit (Matt. 5:3).	Humility	Stripped of pride and sensitive to God's ministry in their behalf.	Isa. 61:1; Luke 4:16–21; 7:22
those who mourn (Matt. 5:4).	Sensitivity	Responsive to personal sinfulness and tenderhearted toward one another.	Isa. 61:2; Eccl. 3:1–8; Luke 19:41; John 11:33, 35
those who are meek (Matt. 5:5).	Meekness	Demonstration of self-control and submission.	Matt. 6:33; 1 Pet. 3:1–7
those who hunger and thirst for righteousness (Matt. 5:6).	Obedience	Desire to hear and do the will of God.	Luke 1:53
those who are merciful (Matt. 5:7).	Compassion	Outworking of faith to meet the needs of others.	Luke 1:58
those who are pure in heart (Matt. 5:8).	Holiness	Lifestyle of set-apartness including thoughts and actions.	Ps. 24:4-6
those who are peacemakers (Matt. 5:9).	Reconciliation	Forbearance instead of retaliation; forgiveness of wrongs; restoration of fellowship.	Rom. 3:25; 12:18; Eph. 4:32; Phil. 1:3–5; Titus 3:2; 1 John 1:7
those who are persecuted for righteousness' sake (Matt. 5:10).	Commitment	Steadfast loyalty that cannot be broken.	Luke 13:35; 2 Thess. 2:15–17; 2 Tim. 2:3
those who are reviled and persecuted (Matt. 5:11).	Patience	Willingness to endure suffering.	1 Pet. 2:19–21; 3:14; Rev. 12:11

Chart by Dorothy Kelley Patterson from *The Woman's Study Bible* (Nashville: Thomas Nelson, 1995).

Notes

1. Matt. 5:3–10.
2. Matt. 5:11–12.
3. Ps. 34:8.
4. Exod. 34:6; Ps. 136:1.
5. 489–425 B.C.
6. Died about A.D. 21.
7. A.D. 23–79.
8. See Eph. 3:8.
9. See 1 Cor. 15:51–52; 2 Cor. 3:18.
10. Matt. 16:24.
11. See Gal. 2:20; James 2:5.
12. Isa. 53:7.
13. Matt. 4:3–4.
14. Matt. 4:5–6.
15. Matt. 4:8–10.
16. See Deut. 8:3; 6:13, 16.
17. "Rock of Ages" by Augustus M. Toplady (1975).
18. Phil. 2:5–8.
19. Matt. 16:24; Luke 1:52; James 4:10; 1 Pet. 5:6.
20. Matt. 8:20.
21. Rev. 14:14.
22. Ps. 9:12; 22:26; 41:1–2.
23. 1872–1968.
24. Died about 480 B.C.
25. Brooke Noel Moore and Kenneth Bruder, *Philosophy: The Power of Ideas* (Mountain View, Calif.: Mayfield Publishing Company, 1990), 575.
26. Rom. 12:3.
27. Matt. 16:24–25.
28. Rom. 12:10.
29. Luke 1:46–55.
30. Luke 1:38.
31. Matt. 23:12.
32. John 14:16; 16:13.
33. Isa. 10:8.
34. 2 Tim. 2:15.
35. Ps. 8:3–5; Matt. 6:28–34.

36. Ps. 119:15–16; Phil. 4:8.
37. "Just As I Am," by Charlotte Elliott (1834).
38. Luke 2:7.
39. Ruth 1:16–17; 4:15.
40. Ruth 1:20–21.
41. See Prov. 24:10; 1 Cor. 1:25; 2 Cor. 12:9.
42. Ruth 3:3.
43. Esther 5:1–2.
44. Prov. 31:22.
45. 2 Cor. 3:2–3.
46. 1 Pet. 3:3–4.
47. 1 Pet. 3:15.
48. See Matt. 5:5–7.
49. "Son of David," Matt. 15:22.
50. "Lord," Matt. 15:25.
51. "Lord, help me," Matt. 15:25.
52. Thomas Watson, *The Beatitudes* (Carlisle, Penn.: The Banner of Truth Trust, 1989), 58.
53. Matt. 6:33; Luke 10:9; 17:21.
54. Luke 11:2; Rev. 11:15.
55. Matt. 16:19; Luke 9:62; 2 Tim. 4:18; Rev. 22:3–5.

Crying in the Chapel

BE SENSITIVE:
LET YOUR ATTITUDE REFLECT
SPIRITUAL SENSITIVITY

The Context: Matthew 5:3–12

**"Blessed are those who mourn,
For they shall be comforted."**

MATTHEW 5:4

Three kinds of "mourning" are found in Scripture: (1) a natural state that comes from personal tragedy;[1] (2) a sinful state in which the sinner refuses to repent and seek forgiveness in order to be comforted;[2] and (3) a "godly sorrow" out of which issues genuine repentance.[3]

The latter—spiritual mourning—is the subject of the second beatitude. These blessed individuals have a sense of their sinful condition issuing from a sensitive conscience and prompted by a broken heart.

Blessedness comes to the Christian woman who is sensitive to sin in her own life and tenderhearted toward sorrows in the life of another. She then becomes aware of her own unworthiness and of her own inability to comfort herself or others. She finds comfort in knowing that her trust is not in herself but in God. Godly sorrow works repentance.

There are mourners whose mourning brings no comfort—for example, the woman who adopts a spirit of pessimism, searching for despair and sorrow as a bee seeks honey. For this woman, to be happy and content is to be miserable and to make everyone else miserable. Also, the woman who sorrows and pouts over some selfish disappointment or thwarted ambition cannot be comforted. Not every woman who suffers the loss of a loved one enjoys the comfort God wants to give. Some become bitter and rebellious toward God. Finally, some mourn only because they have suffered the effects of their own sinfulness. In fact, the human spirit naturally and instinctively withdraws from the suffering or sadness that prompts mourning. Again, the path to blessing is the antithesis of the logic of the world.

Mourning in itself offers no comfort. The comfort is in Christ, who is the source of all comfort.[4] The Greek expression *pentheō* was used by the ancient Greeks to express lamentation and extreme sorrow for the dead. The sorrow referenced here is not just bereavement but the signs of an overwhelming grief. In other words, to mourn is to grieve with a grief that so overwhelms the whole person that it cannot be concealed.

In the New Testament, the word is consistently used to express overt or manifested sorrow.[5] The first step in this spiritual pilgrimage was acknowledging spiritual poverty—the confession of personal sinfulness. Then follows sorrow because of that sin, i.e., contrition.

Again, there is a paradox since most people do not recognize sorrow as being a blessing. Rather, sorrow is considered to be a blight upon the human experience. Leaders of the Christian Science cult even deny the existence of physical illness and other conditions that cause grief. Founded in the mid-nineteenth century by Mary Baker Eddy, this cult believes that healing is effected only by prayer rather than by medical procedures. But this has not erased sorrow and death from its followers. It seems unlikely that the cult would be inviting to converts since it offers no compassionate help to those in sorrow and difficulty. Christian Science practitioners or spiritual leaders rarely visit patients, read the Bible, or pray for healing. The practitioner simply commits to pray for the individual. Many of its followers are losing their faith in the teachings of Christian Science and returning to the temporal care of modern medicine.

Sorrow and death are part of humanity. They will always exist. They will not be abolished in this world, but they can be endured with grace and used to edify the believer when the Holy Spirit walks alongside.[6]

On the other hand, this beatitude does not suggest that all those who sorrow—whether over physical suffering or financial reverses or the loss of a loved one—will be blessed simply because they have suffered grief. This mourning is not the false pseudo-piety of those who feel you have to be miserable to be religious. Unfortunately, the true nature of Christian joy is often missed in a superficial expression of joviality.

Sorrow has been so interwoven into life that even pleasures are often tainted with pain. During the happy and excited planning of our daughter's wedding, my husband and I realized that even this joyous occasion would be marked by the sorrow of separation from our daughter. With the exception of the one year she attended a university in another state, Carmen had lived in our home throughout her life—for twenty-two years.

When Carmen married, she would be moving to live with her husband; her room would be empty; her telephone would not ring; her shower would not awaken me in the morning; her cheerful voice would not greet me in the afternoon; her sparkling eyes and happy spirit would never again be consistently within the walls of our family home. Yet this sorrow did not rob me of joy, but rather it was bathed in the solace that our daughter had fulfilled another purpose in God's plan for her life. And there is more: She brought me another son! Mark is all I could ever want in a son just as is our firstborn Armour. He is a strong and godly young man. He loves God; he loves Carmen; and he even loves me! The deep joy that flows within my heart is more than enough to replace the sorrow of this experience.

The Need for Night Vision

Darkness has long been associated with evil and wickedness,[7] danger and death,[8] confusion and chaos,[9] dreariness and sorrow.[10] On the other hand, light suggests beauty and grace, happiness and joy, brightness and vision. Jesus called Himself the "Light of the world."[11] There is no greater contrast than that between darkness and light. Christ can be seen most clearly in the darkness. In fact, He chases away the darkness by His presence.[12]

When I contemplate the times in my own life when Christ has been most real to me, such times have been the dark hours when I could not see a solution, when the path ahead was dim, when I was at the end of myself and had exhausted my own resources. These were times when weeping would endure for the "night" of sorrow, to be followed by the morning dawn of His light,[13] the "night" of suffering when

I would be accompanied by His song,[14] the "night watches" of soul searching when He was my help.[15] In Christ, the night shines like the day![16]

In fact, my unique personal testimony does not rest in the conversion experience of an eight-year-old girl. Reared in a godly home, active in a soul-winning church, possessed of a heart sensitive to God, I came to know the Lord in quietness and without fanfare. However, giving Him complete control of my life was a desperate struggle—not because I was drawn to the world and its ways but because I was so obsessed with busyness in doing all the things I wanted to do for God that I did not have time to enjoy fellowship with Him and to build my character through Him.

Mary of Bethany chose to learn at the feet of Jesus rather than to look for satisfaction by doing good things in the name of Jesus. Somehow I had missed that lesson. Jesus commended Mary for choosing that which would never be taken away from her—sitting at His feet, being saturated by His Word.[17]

God reached me through a series of sorrows and difficulties. First, a very serious and life-threatening illness resulted in a chronic condition that would "make me to lie down"[18] and demand that I spend time resting my physical body, which, in turn, opened the door for a new experience in resting and meditating in the Word of the Lord. Then came the loss of a baby. Initially, the baby seemed to be coming at an inconvenient time. However, after I felt that life within the womb and then started to lose the baby, I was overwhelmed with the desire for that baby and even found myself demanding of God that I be allowed to keep the baby.

But God never buckles to our demands; He always continues with His master plan; the baby died in the womb. Then I lived as a virtual invalid for a lengthy period, and surgery threatened my fertility. Yet I did give birth to two babies. And, despite the trauma that threatened each fragile life, God spared them both.

In later years, the battle moved to what seemed to be a more intimate human level. The enemy moved into the camp in the sense that
no longer was the suffering endured in the midst of a caring Christian
community in which an inner circle of Christian friends was lifting me
up and fighting with me against the attack launched by the Evil One.
The personal attack upon my husband, his ministry, and his reputation
came not from a pagan community but from those whom we had considered our closest and dearest friends.[19] Those launching the attacks
on our lives were fellow believers.

Never have I read and meditated upon Scripture so much, and
never has the Word been any more quick and powerful to do its work
in my life than during these dark days. My suffering in many ways
seemed to be in isolation. Yet never have I experienced His faithfulness
any more than during these days of physical suffering, emotional
anguish, and spiritual desperation.[20] God did raise up spiritual warriors
to stand with us, but they were not from the innermost circle of those
who had claimed to be our friends.

Yes, never have I seen more clearly the Lord Jesus than during
those days when His presence, and essentially only His presence, illu-
minated and removed the darkness. I drank of the cup of His sufferings as He did in Gethsemane when those closest to Him were indifferent or, in the case of Peter, abandoned Him.[21]

My own sinfulness and unworthiness remained ever before me as I
was amazed at the Lord's protection and comfort during the most difficult days we had ever faced. Our family seemed isolated in the midst
of an assault from some who were a part of the Christian community.
Even more devastating than experiencing the rejection of indifferent
acquaintances is the pain of standing under the secretly mounted
attack of those nearest and dearest "friends"—those who would cast
their arrows and spears with intent to inflict upon you and your family
mortal wounds, while still pretending concern for your well-being.[22]

The Blessing of Sorrow

Perhaps you are asking, *When is suffering a curse and when is it a blessing?* As a gravel walk is crushed with load after load and then walked upon again and again, it becomes harder. Myrrh is crushed in order to release its fragrance. Sorrow will harden some people and make others more fragrant.

Mary Magdalene was a woman who was overwhelmed with her personal sinfulness. Even her name *Mary* (from the same Hebrew root as *myrrh*) means "bitterness." Remember Naomi, whose name meant "pleasant," in the midst of her overwhelming sorrow changed her name to *"Mara"* because, as she expressed it, "The Almighty has dealt very bitterly with me."[23]

Mary's testimony was a tribute to the Lord and His faithfulness to forgive. She had been crushed with the burden of her sin, broken over the tragedies of her life. Yet in her brokenness, she experienced the healing forgiveness of Jesus. Because Mary had experienced such forgiveness personally, she reached out to others with greater sensitivity. Her contrite heart made her a channel for sympathy and comfort to others who were hurting. Just as the crushing of myrrh brings an aromatic fragrance, so the crushing Mary endured was but the beginning of the fragrance of a life molded by obedience in the midst of adversity. Mary Magdalene voluntarily repented. With a heart of gratitude and a spirit of devotion, she humbly served the Savior, following Him even to the cross.

Iris Blue grew up in a Christian home. Her parents not only took her to church, but they also saw that she was involved in all the activities of the church. Yet in her childhood, Iris rejected the faith of her parents. By her early teens she had marred her life with prostitution, drug abuse, and a host of other tragic actions and addictions that led to her imprisonment as a convicted criminal.

Iris's rebellion and belligerence within the prison system only extended her stay there. When she was finally released, she began to operate a bar and house of prostitution; and there someone finally reached out and successfully brought her to Christ. Again and again the witness had been given; invitations to church had been extended. Finally, it was as if a hound of heaven literally dragged her before the Lord, where all the forces of heaven came upon her until she could resist no longer. In her words, "I knelt down on the Houston sidewalk a tramp sinful and dirty, but I got up a lady clean and pure because I was washed in His blood!"

Perhaps the words of Iris Blue could have also been the testimony of Mary Magdalene. Mary, too, was probably lovingly nurtured by her Jewish parents. Yet she, too, made some wrong choices that seemed to ruin her life and destroy all opportunity for happiness. But for Mary Magdalene, Iris Blue, and a host of other women, Jesus has never stopped seeking to redeem and restore. God does indeed use those who have been broken, for they have been through the refiner's fire.[24] The fragrance of the perfume is strong within its vial, but its most intense diffusion occurs when the vial is crushed or broken so that the fragrance escapes its walls and permeates everything around.[25]

Blessedness is not the result of all mourning. Every experience in sorrow does not necessarily mean an automatic blessing. Spiritual mourning is not a one-time experience reserved for the conviction that leads to salvation. The tense of the verb indicates a present and continuing experience. Every believer continues to be plagued with sins of omission and commission. Spiritual mourning indicates a sensitive consciousness of sin and an accompanying sorrow because of that sin.[26]

Since we have already established that this blessedness is a Christlike quality, in order for you to be truly blessed, the Lord Jesus must dwell within your heart. Nevertheless, mourning is another step (following humility) in the ladder to blessedness and an additional condition that prepares you to receive the blessedness God wants to give. Reserves have long been on deposit in the divine bank, but it is up to you to seek the withdrawal based upon your standing as an heir to the heavenly account (i.e., because you have a personal relationship with the heavenly Father who controls the account).

Those who mourn have recognized who they are. In ascending this ladder to blessedness, you begin by going down (acknowledging poverty of spirit or humility). Having humbled yourself before the Lord, you are then ready for the godly sorrow that works repentance.[27] This contriteness of heart is illustrated in the tears that bring us to Jesus. A Christian woman who is blessed can see purpose in sorrow and use that sorrow for the glory of God. Sorrow leads us to Christ; and that sorrow, when carried triumphantly, draws others to Christ most effectively. Sorrow seems to be an integral part of service and obedience.

A Woman's Wisdom

"But I think that for converts—indeed for all Christians— the acknowledgment of sin is not self-hatred at all, but the beginning of self-acceptance and (in the healthy sense) of self-love. The dialogue with God which begins with the confessions of one's own failures is not depressing; it is liberating."

—Emilie Griffin

The right kind of sorrow will always be lost in God's comfort because it ends in Christ.[28] No sorrow can separate a blessed woman from Christ.[29] There is a definite bridge between the blessedness God wants to give and the suffering He permits.[30] A woman who is blessed will see purpose in suffering and sorrow and use these challenges as a path to God's comfort.[31] Also, this sorrow extends beyond grief for your own sins and extends to grief over the sins of others, the church, and the world.[32]

You must not confuse the sorrow of a contrite heart with the sorrow that results from sin, the latter of which brings no blessing.[33] Judas was sorry that things turned out as they did. His outpouring of regret was expressed with the Greek word *metamelomai,*[34] which has the sense of regret. However, genuine "godly sorrow" is described with the Greek word *metanoian* (literally, "second-minded"), which has the sense of a complete reversal of heart and direction.

To recognize your personal sinfulness and helplessness in sorrow or mourning over spiritual failure is an important step toward reconciliation with God. Violation of the laws of God brings suffering and tragic consequences. Jesus is looking for the sorrow arising out of a sanctified and regenerate heart.[35] The former causes despair, as a woman will surely mourn deeply over the consequences of her sin and the heartaches accompanying that sin. On the other hand, the sorrow from a heart sensitive to God brings joy and peace. Sanctified sorrow is grief prompted by the sin itself rather than by the sin's consequences, which have merely affected your lifestyle in an adverse way.[36]

Jesus makes joy the final stanza of every midnight song. Christ, because He is the light, can be seen more clearly in the darkness. Your sorrows are merely a stormy channel through which you must pass to reach the tranquil lake of peace. Unbending steel is iron that has passed through the testing fire; artistic statuary has suffered the blows of hammer and chisel; glittering diamonds have passed through fierce heat. The nightingale sings only in a darkened cage during the day. Even the beautiful rainbow is the result of God's tears.

In my Bible is a laminated photograph of a series of beautiful rainbows taken by my friend Heather at Igaucu Falls in Argentina. During our visit there we had opportunity to do some prayer walks, sharing our burdens with one another and with the Lord. The unique, multicolored series of rainbows seemed to overwhelm us with the presence of the Lord and the assurance that He would be faithful. Some of the challenges we put before the throne of the Lord did not seem to have solutions, but we agreed, standing in the shadow of the rainbow promise, that we had faith in His faithfulness! Every time I come to spend time with the Lord, that photo falls from my Bible. I am reminded again that He is ever present to walk beside me through whatever valley may loom before.

Though your happiness may make you forget to be thankful, your misery often drives you to prayer and communion with the heavenly Father. God neither loves sorrow nor rejoices in your suffering. But He is pleased to see a woman open the latch to Him in her hour of need. He does use sorrow for your good. He brings your suffering and difficulties into the realm of purposeful challenge. What comes as the direct result of sin and evil is turned by God into a crucible for refining.[37]

The word translated *comforted* is from the same Greek root from which the name of the Holy Spirit is derived (Greek *paraklētos*, literally, "one called alongside"). The Holy Spirit is the Comforter because He brings conviction of sin and awakens sorrow over sin; He is the one who enables you to cry out for help.[38]

The woman who mourns because of her sin does so in the power of the Holy Spirit, who abides within as her comfort, joy, and enabler. From your study of English grammar, you will recall that a verb in the active voice expresses an action performed by its subject. A verb in the passive voice expresses an action performed *upon* its subject or describes a situation in which the subject is the result of the action. The use of a verb in the passive voice here suggests that the comfort described does not originate in the sorrow itself or within you; rather, this comfort comes from beyond yourself. You are being acted upon.

Not only is this verb in the passive voice, but it is also in the aorist future tense. This pinpoints not so much the time of the action as the effectiveness of the movement of God in your life. This tense indicates action that is an accomplished fact of the past, together with the dimension of an action that continues to be experienced in the future.

There is not only certainty for the present time but also security for the future. There will be a continuous cycle of comfort through the constant and uninterrupted indwelling of the Holy Spirit within a believing heart.[39] Many women are content to play hide-and-seek with God, hiding from His assignments and commandments and selectively seeking His benefits and rescue. The blessedness for which you are reaching expects and demands His constant, comforting indwelling. Of course, there is also a future dimension to this promised comfort as the day approaches when all people will come face-to-face with the living Lord.

This beatitude is also a paradox in that the world pities those who are caught up in sorrow and shrinks away from mourning. But in the kingdom of heaven the ones who have been called upon to suffer are those favored. Ultimately, the blessedness is not found in the sorrow or mourning itself but in the comfort that accompanies this sorrow. Only God can take evil and misery and make it the condition in which the greatest joy and comfort are found. There are some blessings that cannot be obtained unless you are willing to accept and endure suffering. Even the birth of a baby—one of life's most joyous events—comes after a season of birth pangs, a time of suffering and struggle.

Some years ago the family of one of our colleagues received the chilling news that their eldest son had been stricken with a malignant brain tumor. Luel went through surgeries and other rigorous treatments. We prayed earnestly for divine intervention. He rallied several times, but finally God decided to take the boy home to heaven, giving him complete healing but leaving those who loved him with an overwhelming sense of loss. Releasing him was painful, even beyond the family circle, to those who had watched and loved the boy. Yet in no way could we experience the anguish and pain of the family as the gifted and godly young man's life ebbed away.

During Luel's memorial service, which became a celebration of his life and commitment to Christ, I became acutely aware of the blessing of affliction and suffering as I observed firsthand the spiritual grace and powerful testimony of that family who had been with the Lord and depended upon Him in a way few people ever experience. I saw the battle of faith in the life of my own son Armour, who had loved Luel as a brother and who had walked with him through this dark valley with no understanding of such a tragedy. Not until months later did God use this tragedy to build up Armour's own understanding of God's faithfulness.

One of my dearest friends, a woman committed to the Lord, suffered deeply and for a lengthy period during her valiant battle against cancer. Margaret Baxter never complained; she always lifted up Jesus; she continued to pray faithfully for me in the midst of my trials at a pivotal time in my life; she represented the Lord Jesus with grace and charm to the very end. She was always a woman of God, but I watched her blossom into a genuine heroine of the faith through those months of suffering. I felt her spiritual strength reach out to me and meet my needs in such a precious way. Drinking of the cup of His sufferings will equip you for ministry in an awesome way.

The Tears of Sorrow

Tears need not imply a perpetually sorrowful attitude toward life but rather ought to point to those occasions when a woman is moved to deepest pity and sympathy, especially when the Lord burdens her heart for her sins and for the sins of others.[40] Genuine tears are cleansing, like a raging flood that carries away the rubbish in the aftermath of destruction.[41] In the Christian life there is a ministry of tears. When Jesus wept, His tears were not tears of human weakness but tears of divine compassion.[42] Keith Green, before his untimely death, penned some words I carry in my Bible:

Oh, what can be done for an old heart like mine;
Soften it up; Cleanse me I cry; let my heart break;
Let tears once again flow down my face
For the souls of lost men.

Tears become the outlet for your inability to change men and women and lead them to experience what has made life worth living for you.[43] Tears also may woo back to the Lord your children or other dear ones who have gone astray.[44] Tears of loving concern are a powerful influence for God. How often have Christian mothers wept bitter tears over their wayward sons and daughters. Spiros Zodiates shares a thought that he has preserved on the desk in his study: "Never despair of a child. The one you weep the most for at the mercy seat may fill your heart with the sweetest joys." I believe that with all my heart.

Across the years I have wept with my children, and with a host of young people God has brought across my path, through crisis after crisis. Our children have loved the Lord and have been involved in His fellowship. Neither has been involved in drugs or impure living, but each has had spiritual crises. Each at one time or another has refused my counsel and spiritual guidance, and each has been at some point out of fellowship with the Lord, as have we all. How helpless I have felt in those seasons of rebellion, and how hypocritical I have felt to be engaged in ministering to parents and young people when my own child was not totally committed to serving Christ in purest obedience. Concern can do far more than condemnation, and tears are a precious testimony of loving concern.

Some great authors have penned profound statements on the powerful impact of tears. Washington Irving once said: "There is a sacredness in tears. They are not the mark of weakness, but of power. They speak more eloquently than ten thousand tongues. They are the messengers of overwhelming grief, of deep contrition, and of unspeakable love."[45] Sir Walter Scott compared tears to the softening showers that cause the seed of heaven to spring up in the human heart.[46]

The sweet psalmist David referred to a bottle for tears.[47] I have a lovely framed Isra   rendition of this bottle cross-stitched by my friend Dawn Jones. It hangs in my bedroom. David's reference seems to be to a leather or skin bottle such as those used to store liquids.

Perhaps such a metaphor suggests that the tears are so many that they would need a bottle to hold them! Most commentators see this unusual request as figurative, holding that there is no evidence of any Semitic funeral ritual that called for a collection of tears into a bottle. The latter practice, the wearing of small lachrymatories as an adornment by fashionable Roman women, has also been suggested by some as associated with the long, narrow perfume jars found in graves. Nevertheless, the metaphor is effective in showing how precious these tears are to the Lord and perhaps even to suggest that they are stored for a future use, perhaps as refreshment.

Mary shed her tears at the feet of the Lord;[48] Paul's tears[49] and the tears of the Lord Himself were instruments for bringing a harvest of souls. Tears are an expression of your complete dependence upon God. Tears reach heavenward for the power of God to prevail when your words and your counsel fail. On more than one occasion I have fallen prostrate on the floor of the bedroom of one of our children and bathed the carpet with my tears as I lobbied the sacred throne for divine intervention in the life of one whom I loved more than life itself. My tears were a testimony to my personal frailty and inadequacy and a means of cleansing my heart of its own devices and plans to enable God to come in and do His work unfettered.

The ancient Greeks considered sorrow a sign of weakness. They admired and even worshiped beauty and symmetry of form as their exquisite statuary bears witness. Consequently, they had no time or sympathy with those who sorrowed. Jesus, on the other hand, was a man of sorrows and acquainted with grief, and He came in order to bear your sorrows.[50] He introduced mourning in the Sermon on the Mount as a spiritual discipline. The Lord Jesus moved pain and sorrow from the accidental to the purposeful. He views your pain and suffering in relationship to other things.

Consider a Historical Note

An interesting story is told about the famous opera star Jenny Lind. When the German musician Goldschmidt heard her, he commented to Miss Lind that he could detect a little harshness in her tone. He further suggested that if he could marry her and break her heart, this harshness would disappear. Goldschmidt did later marry Jenny Lind, and he did break her heart. People who heard her in later years said that the bit of harshness had indeed left her voice.[51]

Perhaps no woman's pen has touched more lives than that of Elisabeth Elliot. Her impact on me personally has been beyond any expression. I have been inspired by her life, challenged by her writing, edified by her messages, delighted by her friendship, and encouraged by her fellowship. Yet I remember a most perplexing event when Elisabeth came to Dallas to speak at a conference that I was hosting.

Because of my assignment to oversee the conference as well as to speak each day, I asked my young student intern to serve as Elisabeth's driver and personal hostess. She was delighted and excited over the opportunity. I remember the afternoon Kristi, having met Elisabeth at the airport and delivered her to the hotel, came into my office. She entered crestfallen and forlorn. I inquired as to what disaster might have happened, and she simply said, "She's not what I expected; she's not happy or friendly; I don't think she's going to have much to say."

At first I was caught completely off guard, but I quickly recovered and simply asked Kristi to reserve her judgment until after she had heard Elisabeth speak. For, as I contemplated Kristi's initial impression, I realized that Elisabeth was not a gregarious, outgoing, charismatic personality. In fact, I felt strongly in my heart that she probably would not have survived the sorrows of her life (the trauma of losing two husbands—one murdered in the Ecuadorian jungle and another having painfully and slowly suffered death from cancer) if it were not for her contemplative and meditative personality. How could she have been able to articulate so clearly biblical principles for dealing with such adversities if she had not learned the blessedness that comes from spiritual mourning?

Elisabeth's heart was indeed tender, her feelings deep, and her joy genuine. The wisdom she shared from God's Word came from having drunk of the cup of His sufferings as few others had done. At the end of the week, Kristi had a completely different view as she chatted freely with me about all she had learned from that godly woman! Sensitivity to the Spirit of God has been a character trait of Elisabeth Elliot for many years, and her mourning has not only prompted the comfort of God in her own life but has been a channel for His comfort to others.

Hannah exemplified this character trait in her life when she answered Eli and said, "No, my lord, I am a woman of sorrowful spirit. I have drunk neither wine nor intoxicating drink, but have poured out my soul before the Lord."[52] She wanted a son and refused to give up her desires. Hannah took her petition directly to the Lord. Her sensitive spirit and sorrow of heart surely awakened the compassions and mercies of the Lord and became channels for comfort to her heart and the answer to her petition.

The Hope of Sorrow

Once I was awakened to the unique fragrance of personal sorrow in a unique way. My godly father-in-law went to be with the Lord after a lengthy and debilitating illness. His last few weeks were stressful for all the family because he had reached a point of being unable to do even the most basic bodily functions for himself. He was in constant discomfort and often even in pain.

On the day he died, my husband was preaching in another state. Our daughter had accompanied him. My son was in class. I had been attending a seminar in a nearby city and had to return quickly to the hospital. I went from one responsibility to another and did not reach home until late in the evening. When I opened the door, I was overwhelmed with the fragrant jasmine, which had been delivered to our home in my absence. The flowers were beautifully and appropriately worked into a lovely arrangement sent to our home under the direction of our dear friend Ruth Hunt.

Consider a Historical Note

For years, in the land of Israel, Jewish women have made regular pilgrimages to what they and all the world once called the "Wailing Wall," located at the Temple Mount in the heart of the Old City of Jerusalem. There, especially on the Sabbath, which begins on Friday evening and extends until sundown on Saturday, they would approach the wall with their tears of genuine grief for the tragedies suffered by their people and especially because of their exile from the holy city of Jerusalem. Many still go to this site, but it has a new name. It is now called the "Western Wall" because the tears are now tears of joy and thanksgiving that the Jewish nation once again presides over Jerusalem and that the Jews can worship in freedom at this holy place. Tears do not have to mean despair and hopelessness. Mourning can be the door to a new beginning.

Immediately the Lord ministered to my hurting heart by this subtle reminder that my father-in-law's life had been a fragrance unto the Lord. Even after his passing, his influence still remained to be felt and enjoyed. In death as in life he would continue to touch lives and represent the Lord Jesus. The bitterness of sorrow cannot be separated from human life, but mourning sanctified by the Lord can become the catalyst for the fragrance of testimony, whether in life or death.[53]

God grant that your mourning will not be for naught but will open the door to mending. That is what divine comfort is all about. Someone once suggested that a woman's extremity is God's opportunity.[54] Even sorrow is worthwhile if, in the midst of that grief, you can detect the divine presence of the Lord and feel His power equipping you to accomplish His purposes.[55]

To have your weakness revealed is more often than not a bitter experience, but to experience God's strength is certainly the heart of blessedness. You begin to learn what Christ can do for you when you experience what you cannot do for yourself. Just as surely as there is divine help for human need, there is heavenly comfort for earthly sorrow.

Charles Dickens's story of Little Dorrit includes a vivid description of two men imprisoned in Marseilles. Though they were occupying the same cell, the food served was quite different since one was well-to-do, receiving a more plentiful and varied diet, while the other was very poor. The man with abundance inquired of his cell mate about the taste of his coarse bread, to which the poor man responded, "I can cut my bread so—like a melon. Or so—like an omelet. Or so—like a fried fish." He happily demonstrated how the various cuts were to be shaped and described his imaginary sauce for each morsel. This prisoner had determined to make his mind and attitude triumph over his circumstances. His joy and contentment were not dependent on circumstances or environment and thus could not be taken from him.

Jesus went far beyond this concept as He came "to console those who mourn . . . to give them beauty for ashes, the oil of joy for mourning, the garment of praise for the spirit of heaviness."[56] Believers learn from Jesus that there is a positive way to walk down the paths of life, passing through the darkness as it comes and reaching for the joy of the Lord, which indeed does bring comfort to those who are mourning.[57]

The apostle Paul wrote about the hope that came to him in his deepest despair as he spoke of being hard-pressed on every side yet not crushed, perplexed but not in despair, persecuted but not forsaken, struck down but not destroyed.[58] Jesus' unique pronouncement about the mourning heart has been validated again and again. Only His soothing balm heals the bitter sting and even reaches down to remove the cause for the pain. He has proven that though your heart may be grieved by overwhelming loss, you cannot lose the grace of God that will see you through whatever storms may come.[59]

A Woman's Wisdom

"The mind of a Christian should be always composed, temperate, free from all extremes of mirth or sadness, and always disposed to hear the voice of God's Holy Spirit."

—Susanna Wesley

The unfailing Comforter is a constant companion whose presence is enough to see you through any trial.[60] He comforts in sorrow, sustains in difficulties, and endures through all. He can bring solace to the sorrowing heart;[61] He imparts pardon to the penitent spirit;[62] He offers shelter in every storm through His indwelling presence.[63]

How vivid in my mind is that day in Baptist Hospital in Beaumont, Texas, when I had to tell my darling youngest sister—still a young adult in the university—that despite her surgeries and every treatment medical science could provide, she would have to yield her fertility in order to salvage her own health. Eileen was unmarried and not even dating seriously at the time, but her heart's desire even then was to marry and bear children.

The family did indeed mourn for her and for ourselves, but in that dark hour the God of all comfort came beside us with His presence and peace. The balm from Gilead was sufficient. Some years later Eileen married a preacher who was serving in a ministry to young people. Her first children were those teens, and there were many of them—more than she could count—who looked to her for love and encouragement and counsel. She laughed with them and cried with them; she celebrated with them and mourned with them; she poured herself into their lives as her own maternity had gone through its ebb and flow and now seemingly was gone. But God had other plans!

The Lord opened the door for Eileen and Steve to adopt a baby girl. It seemed that the mourning had passed for a season, but that baby girl developed some physical and behavioral problems. Again we mourned and waited on the God of all comfort. Ever faithful, He intervened with another promise.[64]

Then our special Sarah began to bloom as a happy and sensitive adolescent, having come to know the Lord Jesus as her Savior and having followed Him in believer's baptism at five years of age. Her spiritual sensitivities are amazing; her physical and behavioral problems have faded away. Humanly speaking, this miracle has come primarily because of Sarah's very special and dedicated mother who has poured herself and her maternity into the life of this chosen daughter. Sarah taught her mother spiritual mourning (godly sorrow), and thus she has been the conduit for heavenly comfort to her mother.

Again, to the world this beatitude is a paradox. The philosophy of the world is to forget your troubles and avoid facing difficulties at any cost. Put on a happy face, and smile, smile, smile. Make your own happiness. Entertainment—anything to give people pleasure—is one of the largest and most profitable industries. On the other hand, the Lord promises blessing and happiness to those who mourn. Poverty of spirit is not to be measured in the financial realm but as a spiritual discipline.

Even so, spiritual mourning has nothing to do with the natural sorrows of this world. Rather, it is the determination to approach life and its challenges with a commitment to serious spiritual responsibility.

Certainly there is no effort to suggest that to be religious or spiritual is to be miserable; nor are laughter and rejoicing the only attitudes attractive to non-Christians. Rather, there is an insistence that one of the greatest problems for the human family is a superficiality or the effort to be or to portray something that does not exist instead of looking for a joy from within that arises to control and determine your lifestyle.

Just as a woman must be poor in spirit before she can be filled with the Holy Spirit, she must experience a real sense of sin and sorrow, intense loss, utter helplessness, and complete despair before she can imbibe the true joy of salvation. When a woman sees herself in complete hopelessness, the Holy Spirit can then reveal the Lord Jesus as her perfect satisfaction. This brings genuine joy and complete comfort in the sense of ultimate consolation and encouragement that only God can supply.[65]

Comfort comes only after mourning has done its work in producing repentance and faith in the Lord Jesus. Once mourning has driven you back to Christ, He is ready to forgive so that peace and happiness can return and you can experience His comfort. One leads immediately to the other.

The believer who "mourns" over her sinful condition refuses to occupy herself with staying in tune with the world or adapting herself to its standards. Rather, she "mourns" for the world and its rejection of the Lord and His ways. She determines to be content to do without the peace and prosperity offered by the world, walking away from demanding her own rights to accept what God offers to her.

When a woman mourns because of her own sin—not merely the consequences of that sin—she will be reconciled with God through His gracious forgiveness and subsequent peace. There is also comfort for those who mourn over the sins of others as Paul had a passion for His people.[66] The final comfort is that state of glory that accompanies life in the heavenly kingdom.[67] Earthly mourning will surely be overshadowed by heavenly comfort![68] God wounds before He heals. Blessedness is not found in the mourning or the sorrow that prompted the mourning but in the comfort God brings to overshadow the mourning with His peace.[69]

A Woman's Wisdom

"I have never seen anyone who I thought had committed more sin than I. . . . I never saw the corruption of but one life, one heart—that was mine. I was never so shocked, so disgusted, so disgraced with remorse over any life so much as my own. My heart was the foulest place I ever saw."

—Carry Nation

As a Christian woman, you must be concerned first with your own sinfulness, but you will also see the terrible fruits of sin in others as well as in the society as a whole. You bear responsibility only for your own sinfulness, but you must carry a burden for the sinful world. In the midst of this sorrow, you must look to God alone for your comfort.[70] In your losses, you will find that He is the only restorer.[71] In the midst of life's upheavals, He alone will remain the same.[72] He will remain the source of your joy for every journey.[73] He will present pardon for all penitence.[74] He will provide a safe harbor in the midst of every storm.[75] In short, He alone can be the happiness for every happening in life.[76]

Prayer and Meditation

Just as I am, without one plea,
But that Thy blood was shed for me,
And that Thou bidd'st me come to Thee,
O Lamb of God, I come! I come!

Just as I am, and waiting not
To rid my soul of one dark blot,
To Thee whose blood can cleanse each spot,
O Lamb of God, I come! I come!

Just as I am, tho' tossed about
With many a conflict, many a doubt,
Fightings within and fears without,
O Lamb of God, I come! I come!

Just as I am, poor, wretched, blind;
Sight, riches, healing of the mind,
Yea, all I need in Thee to find,
O Lamb of God, I come! I come!

Just as I am, Thou wilt receive,
Wilt welcome, pardon, cleanse, relieve,
Because Thy promise I believe,
O Lamb of God, I come! I come!

Just as I am, Thy love unknown
Hath broken ev'ry barrier down;
Now to be Thine, yea Thine alone,
O Lamb of God, I come! I come!

—Charlotte Elliott

Moments for Enrichment

A VERSE TO MEMORIZE

"And God will wipe away every tear from their eyes; there shall be no more death, nor sorrow, nor crying. There shall be no more pain, for the former things have passed away" (Rev. 21:4).

ACTIVITIES TO ENHANCE YOUR UNDERSTANDING OF THE TEXT

1. Contrast the human understanding of "mourning" with the biblical use of the word in the Beatitudes.

2. Consider the reason a Christian woman with the joy of the Lord in her heart should "mourn."

3. Use this chart to illustrate the three types of mourning described in the Bible.

Type of Mourning	Biblical Reference

4. List some specific ways you can develop an attitude of mourning and sensitivity in your own life.

My Goal	Ways to Attain the Goal	Challenge from Scripture

Notes

1. Job 2:13; John 11:33–35.
2. Matt. 27:3–4.
3. 2 Cor. 7:10.
4. 2 Cor. 1:3–4.
5. Matt. 9:15; 1 Cor. 5:2; 2 Cor. 12:21; James 4:9; Rev. 18:11, 15, 19.
6. 2 Cor. 1:3–5.
7. 1 Sam. 2:9.
8. Exod. 10:21; Job 3:5.
9. 1 John 2:11.
10. Isa. 8:22; Joel 2:2.
11. Matt. 5:16.
12. 2 Sam. 22:29; Job 29:3; Ps. 18:28.
13. Ps. 30:5.
14. Ps. 42:8.
15. Ps. 63:6; 77:6.
16. Ps. 139:12.
17. Luke 10:41–42.
18. Ps. 23:2.
19. Ps. 41:9.
20. Ps. 41:10–12.
21. Matt. 26:36–40, 69–75.
22. Job 16:20; Matt. 26:47–56.
23. Ruth 1:20.
24. Isa. 48:10.
25. 2 Cor. 1:8–11.
26. See Ps. 119:53; Eph. 2:11.
27. 2 Cor. 7:10.
28. 2 Cor. 1:3–4.
29. Rom. 8:35–39.
30. Isa. 43:2–3.
31. Ps. 63:6–8; 77:2–6.
32. See Jer. 9:1; Ps. 119:136.
33. See 2 Cor. 7:10.
34. See Matt. 27:3; Acts 1:16.
35. Ps. 51:17.
36. Ps. 51:3–4, 7–12.

37. Rom. 8:18, 31–39.
38. John 16:7–11.
39. Eph. 3:16.
40. Ps. 126:5–6; 2 Cor. 2:4.
41. Ps. 56:8–9.
42. John 11:33–36.
43. 2 Tim. 1:3–5.
44. Ps. 6:8–9.
45. America's first professional writer (1783–1859).
46. Scotland's famed poet and novelist (1771–1832).
47. Ps. 56:8.
48. John 11:32–33.
49. Rom. 10:1.
50. Isa. 53:3.
51. Wallace Bassett, *Beatific Verities* (Kansas City: The Western Baptist Publishing Company, 1917), 36.
52. 1 Sam. 1:15.
53. 2 Cor. 3:2–3.
54. 1 Cor. 1:27.
55. 2 Cor. 12:10.
56. Isa. 61:1–3.
57. John 16:20–22.
58. 2 Cor. 4:8–9.
59. Rom. 8:35–39.
60. John 14:16.
61. Isa. 51:12.
62. Isa. 55:7.
63. Ps. 107:28–30.
64. Isa. 54:13.
65. Matt. 11:28; Heb. 12:11.
66. Rom. 10:1.
67. John 14:1–6; Rev. 21:4.
68. Ps. 30:5b.
69. Phil. 4:7.
70. John 14:18.
71. 2 Cor. 5:17.
72. Heb. 13:8.
73. Neh. 8:10.
74. 1 John 1:9.
75. Ps. 107:28–30.
76. Ps. 144:15.

✤ 3 ✤

Who's in Charge?

BE MEEK:
LET YOUR ATTITUDE BE HARNESSED WITH SELF-CONTROL

The Context: Matthew 5:1–12

"Blessed are the meek,
For they shall inherit the earth."

MATTHEW 5:5

The Beatitudes separate the believer from the nonbeliever precisely because the character traits suggested in this passage and praised in the heavenly kingdom are in opposition to the behavior prompted by the philosophy of the world. The world worships and extols all power—whether military, political, economic, technological, or academic. The world's stereotype of success is not Jesus' model for kingdom citizenship. You might think that the Beatitudes turn the world's values upside down. However, perhaps you should reframe that thought and say that Jesus gave the Beatitudes as a means to turn the world right side up with a view to the heavenly kingdom!

An Inner Virtue That Comes Out

The word *meekness* describes a submissive spirit, i.e., an inner attitude of genuine humility that paves the way to outward service to others. Essentially, a meek woman sees herself as she is—her attitudes, her own sinfulness, her unworthiness, in her own strength, to stand before a perfect God. Her focus moves from dependence upon her own gifts and abilities to her dependence upon God. It is as if she is standing empty-handed before the Lord. Meekness is not a physical condition but a spiritual attitude. It is easier to be honest about your shortcomings when alone before God than to acknowledge your sinfulness before other people.

Have Thine Own Way

Have Thine own way, Lord!
Have Thine own way!
Thou art the potter,
I am the clay!
Mold me and make me
After Thy will
While I am waiting,
Yielded and still.

Have Thine own way, Lord!
Have Thine own way!
Wounded and weary,
Help me, I pray!
Power, all power
Surely is Thine!
Touch me and heal me,
Savior divine!

Have Thine own way, Lord!
Have Thine own way!
Search me and try me,
Master, today!
Whiter than snow, Lord,
Wash me just now,
As in the presence
Humbly I bow.

Have Thine own way, Lord!
Have Thine own way!
Hold o'er my being
Absolute sway!
Fill me with Thy Spirit
Till all shall see
Christ only, always,
Living in me.

—Adelaide A. Pollard

A meek woman seeks to please the Lord. She is totally unconscious of bearing the mark of humility on her life. She gladly obeys the commands of the Lord and cheerfully submits to the authorities God has placed over her. She has no other desire than that God would mold her life according to His design and purpose. Even though I can't remember a day when I didn't love Jesus and wanted to serve him, the pursuit of submitting to the Lord is a constant challenge in my own life.

Meekness (Greek *prautes*), a quality suggesting the self-control of life and actions and submission to the authority of Christ, is honored in Scripture.[1] In each of these Old Testament references, the person—whether the prophet Moses or some unnamed follower of Yahweh—is described as "humble," "lowly," "meek," "poor," or even, in a figurative sense "depressed," in mind or circumstances.

Most inner virtues like meekness have an outward significance. An individual characterized as "meek" is gentle, courteous, kind. However, meekness goes beyond this gracious manner. This character quality suggests a Christian virtue that is free from pretense, self-sufficiency, arrogance, and self-will. Meekness also presupposes humility and sub-missiveness as you recognize that God's thoughts are beyond yours and His ways higher than yours.[2]

Finally, meekness is patient and not resentful. You cannot learn without a spirit of meekness since you must know that you do not know everything in order to learn something you should know.

A Woman's Wisdom

"Women in silence are the listening church, which the teaching church must again and again become."

—Charlotte von Kirschbaum

The biblical term *meekness* denotes someone who is "pleasant," "mild," or "gentle." In fact, the *Oxford Dictionary* makes the specific reference to "Biblical Gr. *praos.*" Interestingly, the dictionary also noted the expression "the gentle sex" as referring to the female sex.[3]

The mild and soothing manner of a person marked by meekness is to be expected as marking the relationships among friends, as describing the demeanor of benevolent rulers toward their subjects, and even as characterizing the attitudes of masters toward their household pet. This deliberate and active attitude suggests a determined, patient endurance that is self-directed rather than a passive or coercive submission forced by the will of another. Meekness is the opposite of roughness, bad temper, or sudden and volatile anger.

In the Old Testament, parallel to the secular classical usage of the word, *meekness* or *gentleness* is used to describe Moses[4] and David[5] and even Ahasuerus.[6] The word cannot exclusively suggest nonviolence since Moses, in his resistance to Pharaoh's oppression of the children of Israel, killed an Egyptian.[7] Rather, the meaning in a spiritual sense would seem to suggest more of a spiritual quality involving total submission to God and utter humility in dealing with other people.

In the classical period, the word *meekness* was used to describe a calm and soothing disposition, in contrast to a temperament marked by rage and savagery, and to imply a moderation that would permit and even encourage reconciliation. Further, meekness maintains serenity in the midst of whatever misfortunes may come, bearing them calmly and patiently. In a secular setting, the word suggests a smiling countenance, a soft voice, a calm demeanor. The person pictured would be accommodating and affable, courteous and kind, charming and gracious, quiet and reserved, easygoing and friendly to everyone.

Among the Greeks this quality was valued highly, especially when accompanied by compensating strength. For example, admired rulers were expected to be gentle with their subjects but firm with their enemies. I once heard an interesting description of the horse of the Greek general Alexander the Great. The magnificent creature was so powerful that no one could stay on his back, much less ride him. Yet the story goes that when Alexander settled into the saddle, the horse was "meek" for his master. The horse chose when to exhibit noteworthy gentleness and obedience, but he did so only when Alexander was in the saddle.

The biblical pattern for a meek and submissive woman is not one in which strength is absent. Quite the contrary. It takes a woman of strength to maintain the God-control in her life that makes possible the bringing of personal desires into subjection to divinely appointed authorities. For example, nothing suggests that a wife is to submit to every male; rather, her divinely assigned responsibility is to submit herself to the leadership of her own husband "as to the Lord."[8] The world looks at submission as a mark of weakness; God considers this spirit of self-control as a hallmark of spiritual strength.

Meekness demands unusual strength. It is not synonymous with weakness. A weak woman may be a doormat just as a weak man may be a wimp. But a woman with genuine meekness exhibits a spiritual strength that overshadows any physical weakness. No woman can be adept at self-control without God-control in her heart. She must be a woman of strength to keep her life on the high plain of godly living.[9]

A Word of Wisdom

"Nothing is so strong as gentleness;
Nothing so gentle as real strength."

—Francis de Sales

Meekness that degenerates into self-abasement is considered inappropriate and unwise. However, a woman marked by a humble attitude of self-control maintains patience regardless of offenses suffered. She is untainted by the vindictiveness or malice of someone else.[10]

Meekness as the Path to Might

Though the opposite of self-aggressiveness and violent self-assertion, meekness in no way suggests servility or servitude. Rather, a meek woman's self-repression is the result of her gracious spirit.[11] She is walking a broad and inclusive path to unselfish ends as she seeks to minister to her family and others whom God brings to her. She does not choose narrow paths to selfish ambition and personal gain.

Meekness does not occur in the Gospels as a word specifically used to name a person, place, thing, or idea. However, the term is used sparingly and carefully as an adjective of description in Matthew 5:5 and 1 Peter 3:4. Its usage in the New Testament context does not suggest the exalting of a sociological condition. Rather, it commends a spiritual condition of submission to and confidence in God, which then unfolds into a lifestyle marked by patience and gentleness.

Meekness describes selfless service to others, not selfish assertion of personal rights. It is associated with humble labor rather than proud ambition. Confident courage is put on deposit, but self-interest is not an option for withdrawal. On the other hand, natural or fleshly meekness is void of spiritual sensitivities and is thus easily deterred from good and even persuaded to evil, in which case it becomes a character defect. Consider Eli, who did not restrain his own children.[12] The prophet who had served the Lord so faithfully in training Samuel, the son of Hannah and Elkanah, did not exercise spiritual leadership with his family and thus failed miserably in managing his own household.

Winsome meekness or gentleness is described as more influential than outward physical beauty or an eloquent verbal testimony. In fact, it is described as the most effective tool for winning an unbelieving husband to Christ.[13] In meekness, the gaining of self-control often means the losing of personal rights. Though meekness may, and often does, demand great personal sacrifice of worldly possessions or earthly position, the apostle Peter notes in return the gain of "that which is very precious in the sight of God."[14]

Paul proved that strength and meekness are compatible. This "man of steel and velvet" used the word *meekness* to describe the correction that he as an apostle planned to bring to the wayward Corinthians.[15] Paul's discipline of his spiritual children was administered without arrogance, impatience, or anger. The apostle assumed for himself the meekness of Christ, which had its basis in love rather than weakness.[16] He reminded believers that correcting their opponents with gentleness might even be a tool for bringing about their conversions.[17]

The Perfect Model

When Jesus described the meek or gentle ones as those who would inherit the earth,[18] He noted this quality as a mark of spiritual maturity and an indication of responsiveness to God's Spirit.[19] Jesus described Himself as "gentle" or "meek,"[20] and yet He is also called the "Lion of Judah" to whom God the Father has committed all judgment.[21]

Jesus did not speak of a discipline foreign to Himself since He is described in the Gospels as "gentle and lowly." Meekness seems inseparably linked to lowliness[22] and gentleness[23] as well as to God's Word and His ways.[24] Before Jesus' incarnation He was presented in prophecy as "meek" or "gentle" and "lowly."[25] Accounts of His life describe Him in the same way during the days of His incarnation.[26] Of course, the spirit of meekness, a right and godly attitude for anyone—male or female—often caused Jesus to endure wrong and ungodly responses, such as contempt and ridicule.

Meekness in the Gender Lens

A woman in her position as a wife is able to reflect the position of the believer to Christ in a unique way. She acknowledges her position in respect of her husband, not because of the demands of human law but because God Himself assigned the wife to be a helper to her husband. Some have found tension in the possibility of a difference between virtues as assigned in a general way to all Christians and virtues appropriated by gender (i.e., because you are a man or a woman).

A careful look at Scripture suggests that rather than different virtues for men and women, there is a difference in how these common virtues are applied individually—whether in timing or degree. In both Ephesians 5 and 1 Peter 3, the instruction given for submission is

addressed specifically to wives and not to husbands. The application of
the teaching occurs within the domestic setting.

A husband esteems his wife as a wife esteems her husband. But
the directive given to wives consistently throughout Scripture frames a
wife's appropriate response to her husband in such a way that her submission to her husband becomes a benchmark in their unique relationship to one another.[27] This submission is mutual only in the sense that
no one has absolute personal autonomy. A husband is not licensed for
self-determination. He, too, has been assigned by God to perform certain duties to his wife, in other words loving her as Christ loved the
church and leading her with a servant's heart.

A husband does not submit to his wife in the same way that she
submits to him any more than Christ is to submit to the church in the
same way the church submits to Him. Rather, a husband submits to his
wife by a willingness to provide, protect, and lead her even at the cost
of his life just as Christ loves and leads the church even to the point of
laying down His life.

Accordingly, the meekness and quietness that characterize the spirit
of a woman are uniquely illustrated within marriage in a wife's obedience
to the divine directive that she submit to her own husband. Nevertheless,
meekness is a "fruit of the Spirit" and thus a reflection of the character of
God in the believer's life.[28] Consequently, those who are meek or gentle
will be true heirs to the inheritance of God.[29] Strength submitted to God
and sanctified by Him works itself out as service to others. Men, too, are
encouraged to model this "fruit of the spirit," or "gentleness,"[30] especially
in the way a husband treats his wife.[31]

For whatever reasons, God issues His directive with purpose and
planning, as well as a unique orderliness.[32] Those whom He created
may not understand what He is doing and the why or wherefore of
what He demands.[33] A man and woman may receive the same spiritual
challenge and yet appropriate it in different ways, according to the
respective role assignment each has been given by God.

The character qualities any woman is called upon to emulate would commonly be understood as *de facto* Christian virtues and thus ideals for all believers. By the same token, however, women are sometimes specifically addressed in Scripture. In those cases the message must have a special application to them.

For whatever reasons, Peter specifically challenged women to seek a "meek and quiet spirit," and he described this attitude as "precious in the sight of God."[34] The virtue of meekness is described by some as especially prized in women. In the Epistle of 1 Peter a lofty challenge is offered to women. Peter's words echo the message of the apostle Paul in his writings.[35]

The imperishable beauty of a "meek and quiet spirit" enables a wife to submit to her husband's authority, even if he is an unbeliever. She knows that God Himself has challenged her to this course of action and that her obedience is to Him.[36] Sarah's husband Abraham was not an unbeliever, but even in uncertain, unpleasant, and dangerous situations she chose to submit to her husband and trust God.[37] There is no basis to suggest that Moses or Peter taught that wives should obey their husbands blindly in whatever a husband instructed his wife to do. Though a wife's model for her submission to her husband is her submission to Christ, submitting to a husband is never portrayed as being the same as or equal to submission to Christ. Wives must obey God first and foremost,[38] but a wife's submission to her husband is a command from the Lord!

Peter did not imply that this meek and gentle attitude will prohibit suffering; rather, he acknowledged that suffering will come.[39] Yet the clear message is that spiritual strength, coming from self-control prompted by God-control within the heart, can and will overcome discouragement and even physical weakness.[40] You dare not run from adversities, for they become God's universities. You cannot escape trials, for they are the fabric into which the threads of your life will be woven. You cannot avoid suffering, for it will bring the fragrance of

Christ to your testimony. Whatever else is involved, certainly submission is the yielding of oneself to the authority and direction of another—an attitude that would be impossible without a "meek and quiet" spirit.

The "meek and quiet spirit" exhibits a dependence upon the Lord and the courage to obey His directives even in the midst of the uncertainties of living with an unbeliever. Such human meekness does not preclude godly boldness. Rather, the meekness is founded upon unwavering confidence in the Lord as the One who enables you to stand for right even in the midst of overwhelming difficulties.[41]

Boldness, as presented in Scripture, is not a reference to obnoxious or aggressive behavior, nor is it the result of personal self-determination. Rather, it is the result of God's work within the human heart. As such, it is a gift that can bring God's Word to the forefront to address those with whom you seek to share a word of divine wisdom—a gift to be sought by every believing woman.[42] Rahab the prostitute acted boldly to provide an escape for the Israelite spies and thus deliverance for God's people. Because she did so, God included her and her family in His deliverance.[43] He even gave Rahab a place of honor in the lineage of Messiah.[44]

Abigail, whose husband was a godless fool, made a bold personal appeal to David and in so doing saved the lives of her household[45] and eventually became a queen.[46] Meekness and boldness are not antithetical. Boldness prompted by your confidence in God and kept within the boundaries the Lord has set is a beautiful and effective accompaniment to meekness. A woman marked by boldness that has been tempered with meekness can accomplish great things for God and receive His blessing in so doing.

A Woman's Wisdom

The wife of the Great Awakening preacher Jonathan Edwards is described by her biographer with these words: "When she herself labored under bodily disorders and pains, which was not infrequently the case, instead of troubling those around her with her complaints, and wearing a sour or dejected countenance, as if out of humor with everybody and everything around her because she was disregarded and neglected, she was accustomed to bear up under them not only with patience but with cheerfulness and good humor."

—Elisabeth Dodds

Queen Esther of ancient Persia is a striking example of biblical "meekness." She was winsome, grateful, selfless, obedient, and courageous.[47] She did experience challenging difficulties. She was a member of a minority race, a girl bereft of father and mother, an alien uprooted from family and friends, a young woman who was saddled with awesome and fearful responsibility. Nevertheless, Esther first submitted herself to her cousin Mordecai, who acted as a foster parent and reared her as his own daughter;[48] she then humbled herself before the keeper of the royal harem—a eunuch (an emasculated man) and a mere "slave" of the king.[49] She subjected herself to Ahasuerus, the pagan monarch who became her husband. She earned his respect, and as a result his heart and ears were open to her.[50]

Through all the events of her life and the relationships she sustained in the process, Esther rose to the occasion with inner beauty and unshaking commitment to God's providence. God used not only her beauty and intelligence but also her meekness and self-control, which were exhibited in the respectful attitude she assumed. Esther knew that ultimately her submission was to the Lord. The Lord not only asked Esther to place herself willingly under the various authorities in her life, but He even asked her to put her own life on the line for her people—the supreme sacrifice anyone can be asked to make.[51]

In meditating upon the life of Queen Esther, you can conclude that Esther did not become the means God used to rescue people through her position and power as the queen of Persia. Rather, God used her meekness and self-control as a submissive wife to touch the heart of her pagan husband. Even the king, according to Persian law, could not reverse his own decrees, and certainly no young queen could do so. The text seems to indicate that the opportunity for Queen Esther to use her creativity and influence came because of the king's love for her, which surely must have been awakened and enhanced by her meek and submissive spirit.

Ahasuerus willingly delegated to Esther the powers of his throne, which, in turn, enabled her to protect her people and accomplish the deliverance God had planned for the Jews.[52] Even the most insignificant events and ordinary happenings of the world are appointed by God to effect His purposes. The personal battle for this quality of meekness is one worth a woman's full commitment.

I have made some tough choices in my own life. In light of my academic preparation, doors opened for the personal pursuit of some very interesting career options. A very challenging conflict has often raged in my own heart because of the priorities that have continually prompted me not only to do the right things for the Lord but also to do them at the right time.

Early in our marriage, I made a choice to be a "helper" to Paige Patterson and to follow his leadership. That choice would require me to bypass some challenging and worthwhile pursuits. In fact, I make choices every day on whether to do what I want to do or to make my personal goals and opportunities subservient to those of my husband. The fact is that in the process of choosing to help my husband I do many things I want to do and go many places I want to go. Meekness for me means giving sensitive consideration to my husband's schedule and needs. Waiting (self-control made possible through God-control) for my husband and working around his schedule is not easy, but it is necessary for me to fulfill my responsibility to him and to the Lord.

No one can live out the Sermon on the Mount without the enabling power of Christ within her heart.[53] The presentation of the foundation is laid in this sermon for the Lord's "new commandment."[54] It is also restated and amplified throughout the New Testament.[55] This "new commandment" challenges believers to love one another even as Christ loved them.

The Sermon on the Mount describes how believers are to do this Christlike loving. Not only do these Beatitudes tell Christians how to live, but they also point back to the gospel and the grace that delivered this gospel. Nothing will drive you to see your ultimate need of the salvation and the unmerited favor with which such grace was delivered any more than the study of this sermon.

The Beatitudes point to your personal helplessness. Just as they seem to crush you, Christ is there to lead you into blessedness. No longer will you be driven by your own desires. Rather, you will be filled with the life of Christ and renewed with His mind—and this is the foundation for glorious happiness.[56] The Sermon on the Mount is a direct road to blessing. Through its principles you can experience demands and implications that will draw you to the discipline essential for living the Christian life. Individuals act on their own, but God knows those actions even when they are mere thoughts. He appoints them to be used for His purposes.

The Laboratory of a Life

Any appeal of the gospel in terms of changing a lifestyle and altering ethical convictions must be based on the assumption that those being addressed are already born-again believers. You cannot expect Christian conduct from a person who is not born again. You cannot make deductions for how you are to live based upon doctrine until the doctrine itself is first presented. Thus, this sermon is addressed to believers.

Although the individual parts of this Sermon on the Mount are important, the spirit behind the whole sermon must also be considered. For example, a woman who teaches the Bible may do so with great eloquence. She may not make factual mistakes; she may be exhaustive in her presentation of historical data; she may even explain the text itself with great accuracy. Nevertheless, if her life and heart are far from the words she has presented, the meaning will be distorted and the application of its teachings lost. Her oratory may be stirring, but her ministry will not bear fruit.

Likewise, if you find something in the Sermon on the Mount that seems wrong for you—a view with which your spirit refuses to agree—then you need to examine your own spirit. Miriam, an extremely gifted woman used of God in an extraordinary way, ended her life and ministry on a tragic note. She allowed pride and rebellion to enter her heart when she spoke against her brother Moses, whom God had appointed to lead the people. Moses was described in the midst of this confrontation as "humble" bearing patiently the insults of his siblings Aaron and Miriam; but the picture of Miriam is one of selfishness and self-centeredness.[57]

You cannot pick and choose which qualities you wish to incorporate into your life. It is all or nothing. The Lord, through His teaching of these attitudes, expects believers to appropriate all of them into their lives. He not only meant them to be taught but also expected them to be "walked" or put into practice. Jesus Himself lived the

Sermon on the Mount. Every woman who has been greatly used of God has taken the Sermon on the Mount seriously. In other words, Jesus says what He means and means what He says! A woman sensitive to Him and committed to His teachings is to be congratulated and admired, for she will achieve genuine happiness and pass on this happiness to others.

These challenging teachings were presented by the Lord as His design for the Christian life. You cannot argue against these principles; you dare not seek to make them ridiculous or out-of-date; you should not distort them or make them appear impossible. Rather, you must bring yourself under the scrutiny of these ideals, molding your own life to their principles.

A Woman's Wisdom

"People before things, people before projects; family before friends; husband before children; husband before parents; tithe before wants; Bible before opinions; Jesus before all."

—Jo Ann Leavell

Unfortunately, though the whole world is longing for and seeking happiness, there is no widespread distribution of happiness. In fact, to read the newspapers and to listen to general media presentations, you would be convinced that there is more misery than bliss abounding on every hand. People tend to seek happiness by evading difficulties and responsibilities. The resulting pseudo-happiness is fleeting and temporary. Henry Drummond expressed it this way: Half the world is on the wrong scent in the pursuit of happiness. . . . They think it consists of having and getting, and in being served by others.[58]

The Guideposts Along the Way to Happiness

Reading the Beatitudes gives you a blueprint that describes what Christian women are to be like (i.e., all Christian women and not just the heroines of the faith). Some have been guilty of trying to divide women into two groups—women of God who are extraordinary on the public platform or with the author's pen on the one hand and those who are ordinary women in the pew on the other. The Scripture offers no such prescription of personality for the elite but presents character qualities for all.

In the New Testament, believers are called "saints," canonized by the Lord in heaven and not by a church on earth.[59] To suggest that only a chosen few are to reach heavenly heights of blessedness while the rest are relegated to live in the earthly lowlands of mediocrity is to deny the heart of the Sermon on the Mount and especially the message of the Beatitudes.[60]

These principles of character are meant for all Christian women; all Christian women are meant to appropriate all of these characteristics. The Beatitudes were never meant to be a cafeteria line from which you pick and choose according to personal whim or convenient season. Some Christian women will be more faithful in developing these qualities and some will show more effectiveness in one than another. But this does not indicate that a *laissez faire* mentality should become the *modus operandi* by human fiat. Though your imperfections will remain, you are still under command to work toward perfection by pursuing all these characteristics. Each beatitude builds upon the previous one and presupposes the one to come.

A Condition from Which You Never Recover

The "blessedness" offered by the Lord includes all the good you could hope to achieve on your own and much more. It is a permanent joy that is not affected by the ups and downs of life. In fact, this joy serves to overshadow and overwhelm the tragedies of life!

Consider this Grammatical Note

The word blessed *occurs eight times in verses 3 through 10 of Matthew 5, and in the original Greek text no verb accompanies it. This prescription for blessedness cannot be given until you have committed your life to Christ. The commandment is not that you are to be blessed but rather that you are to fulfill the conditions that open you to the blessed state. This degree of blessedness is determined by your fulfillment of the conditions set forth by the Lord in the Sermon on the Mount. To fulfill only one condition provides you with only a fraction of the blessedness He offers.*

The Beatitudes are statements of fact concerning the cause and effect of the Christian life. For example, if you do not eat, you will be hungry; and as a natural consequence, you may eventually die of starvation. Here the natural consequences of wrong attitudes or the absence of right attitudes in the Christian life becomes evident. Such would be nonsensical to the non-Christian, but to the citizens of the kingdom of Christ they are edifying indeed. Though the world's happiness depends upon circumstances and their outworking in life, the Christian's blessedness depends upon God and His promises.

For the Christian woman, the right motivation and inner attitude surpasses favorable conditions and outward activity. The more your *heart* seeks to please Him, the less your *body* has to work out deeds to please the Lord. By no means am I suggesting that a *right heart* (governed by the "fear of the Lord") will not prompt the body to do the *right works* (Christ-honoring deeds). With a right heart you please Him without depending upon your own efforts, and you are more blessed in resting in Him than in working for yourself, in letting His

Spirit direct your energies rather than charging forward in your own busyness.[61]

Don't miss in the admonition of James the role of "meekness," which suggests a call for *self-control* in order to prepare the way for *God-control* through the divinely "implanted word"—a word that not only will "save your souls" but also will redeem your actions!

The genuine Christian woman, whose attitudes are described in the Sermon on the Mount, is blessed in her life not because of what happens to her but often despite what happens to her. Joni Eareckson Tada is a woman whom I greatly admire. In a tragic diving accident in her youth, Joni went from an active athlete to a sedentary paraplegic. To observe her from a human perspective awakens pity and prompts the conclusion that Joni Tada has been cursed of God because of her debilitating afflictions of paralysis and helplessness.

Yet from Joni's own lips and from an observation of the ministry of her life, you get the idea that she considers herself blessed. From observing her flourishing creativity, intimate marriage, abundant gifts, and spiritual wisdom, I would agree that the blessings of God rest upon her. Joni's blessed state was certainly not determined by the tragic circumstances of her life. Rather, it resulted from the joyous commitment she made and keeps to the living Lord.

Many women bear handicaps and afflictions that cannot be explained in this life. Their sorrows and burdens are beyond human understanding. God does not measure usefulness to the kingdom and the worth of ministries to others as we tend to do from our human perspective. What we, under the staggering burden of handicapping affliction, view as little accomplishment takes on new meaning when filtered through the divine lens. Sometimes these burdens turn out to be blessings in disguise.

Joni Tada would be quick to agree that she has touched more lives, written more life-changing poetry and books, painted more God-honoring paintings, and turned more people to Jesus since her tragic accident than before. Her life bears overwhelming evidence that God has always been in control of the events in her life. As the blessed controller of all things, the Lord will never abandon His children.[62] Though the Lord may lift His hand for a time to permit you to walk through a dark valley, He is always there in the shadows to see you through.[63] In fact, the key thought in Isaiah's comforting prophecy of encouragement is the word *through*.[64]

Surely Joni Tada and any other women who suffer from handicaps or afflictions look forward to the complete healing heaven will bring,[65] but Joni's blessedness is not held in check until the heavenly state. Her commitment here on earth is a prelude to what she can expect in heaven. You can thank the heavenly Father that He is working within your failure, loss, sorrow, or suffering.[66] You can live triumphantly in a dark and hurting world because you have the light of Christ within.[67]

The blessedness after death will come as an extension of the blessedness here on earth. In fact, heavenly blessedness is the harvest of what has been sown on earth.[68] This blessedness is not something to be sought from God or given by God at your request; rather, it is the result and fulfillment of your obedience to certain conditions that the Lord Himself has set before you. Happiness is the result of your subjective evaluation; blessedness is the result of the Lord's objective choice.

The Inheritance Promised

Inheritance of the land for Israel was an expression of God's intervention and deliverance.[69] To inherit the earth becomes a temporal manifestation of the heavenly kingdom to come and another initiative for expressing God's sovereign rule in history.[70] The spirit of meekness is the key that enables a woman to get enjoyment from this earthly portion, for contentment is a by-product of meekness. The meek have greater enjoyment of the present life on earth because they have a God-given spirit of contentment.[71] God provides for us better than we would provide for ourselves.

There is also a sense in which inheriting the land is enjoying the peculiar blessings of God's people as "joint-heirs" in Christ.[72] The promised legacy of the land reflects equal participation in the coming kingdom of God.

To maintain the happiness that expresses itself in contentment even with the burden of past heartaches and present difficulties, you must learn to rest in future hope. This task is beyond the best of human efforts; it is dependent upon divine resources. The earthly realm is the setting for what is actually a spiritual battle. This genuine happiness rests between the disciplined action of moving forward, saying, "I have learned to be content," and the resting confidence willing to wait on the Lord because "I can do all things through Christ."[73]

The blessings that you ask of the Lord in prayer have nothing to do with this blessedness about which the Lord is speaking here in the Sermon on the Mount. Your asking for the blessings of God presupposes a realization of your own sinfulness and emptiness. This is your way of asking God for His favor and grace. In a sense you are asking the Lord to personalize His blessings by making His promises applicable to you individually.

In the divine economy, the poor will be rich; the mourners will find comfort; the meek will inherit everything. In other words, what is considered weakness by the world is affirmed as strength by heaven. What the world calls wretched and hopeless, Jesus praises as wonderful and meaningful. Charles Wesley said it well: "I think it my highest privilege to be an assistant to all but the head of none." I might paraphrase for my own testimony, "I find it quite satisfying to be a helper to my husband, a nurturer to my children, and servant to all."

God's work of grace begins with poverty of spirit—a sense of personal insufficiency and unworthiness— followed by mourning or sorrow over your sinfulness, and then climaxing in a receptive heart and the breaking of your own willfulness. Then and only then can you be molded and directed in God's ways.[74] Generally this attitude of meekness is a great challenge even to the most gifted and motivated women. It is often the difference between the good and the best.

Meekness is not a natural attitude; rather, it is a supernatural character quality produced by the Spirit of God. Meekness means to stand under His Word, to submit to His discipline, and to commit to going His way. Meekness is submission; it is strength that is voluntarily under God's control. Control does not necessitate weakness. It often takes more strength to exert control over your emotions and responses than to "let it all hang out" according to what seems natural and pleasing to you. Self-control is good, but God-control is better!

Prayer and Meditation

*May I always remember that the bearing of His cross must
come before the wearing of my crown.
His deliverance is not based on what I do but on what He
Himself has already done on the cross.
My rewards come not for works I have done but from my
consistent obedience of His commandments.
My dwelling on earth is temporary; I eagerly anticipate
the transition to my heavenly home.
Meanwhile, my weakness is ever before me until He
covers it with His strength.*

Moments for Enrichment

A VERSE TO MEMORIZE

"Do not let your adornment be merely outward—arranging the hair, wearing gold, or putting on fine apparel—rather let it be the hidden person of the heart, with the incorruptible beauty of a gentle and quiet spirit, which is very precious in the sight of God" (1 Pet. 3:3–4).

ACTIVITIES TO ENHANCE YOUR UNDERSTANDING OF THE TEXT

1. Consider how an adequate view of your own personal sinfulness is necessary to achieve meekness.
2. Distinguish between pride and self-confidence on one hand and boldness and God-confidence on the other.
3. Consider the difference between blind (or personal) vs. focused (or God-inspired) ambition.
4. Contrast the world's view of success with the biblical pattern for personal fulfillment.
5. Describe a servant leader who has had influence in your life.

6. Chart your path from weakness to strength.

My Weakness	Can Become God's Strength	Biblical Reference
A Critical Spirit	Spiritual Discernment	1 Cor. 12:7–11

Notes

1. See also Num. 12:3; Ps. 22:26; 25:9; 37:11; 147:6; 149:4; Isa. 11:4; 29:19.
2. Isa. 55:8–9.
3. *Oxford English Dictionary* (1989): 559–560.
4. Num. 12:3.
5. Ps. 132:1.
6. Esther 5:1.
7. Exod. 2:12.
8. Eph. 5:22.
9. Cf. Prov. 31:10–31.
10. Matt. 5:5; 21:5; James 1:21; 3:13; 1 Pet. 3:4, 15.
11. Rom. 12:10.
12. 1 Sam. 3:13.
13. 1 Pet. 3:1–4.
14. 1 Pet. 3:4.
15. 2 Cor. 10:1.
16. 1 Cor. 4:21.
17. 2 Tim. 2:25.
18. Matt. 5:5.
19. Gal. 5:23.
20. Matt. 11:29.
21. Matt. 21:12; John 5:22.
22. Matt. 11:29; Eph. 4:1–2.
23. 2 Cor. 10:1; Titus 3:2.
24. James 1:20–21; see also Ps. 25:9.
25. Isa. 53:7; Zech. 9:9.
26. Matt. 11:29; 21:5; John 3:3–15; Phil. 2:5–8; 2 Cor. 10:1; 1 Pet. 2:23.
27. Eph. 5:22; Col. 3:18; Titus 2:5; 1 Pet. 3:1.
28. Gal. 5:22–23.
29. Matt. 5:5.
30. Gal. 5:22.
31. 1 Pet. 3:7.
32. 1 Cor. 14:40.
33. Isa. 55:8.
34. 1 Pet. 3:3–4.
35. Eph. 5:22–24; Col. 3:18; Titus 2:4–5.
36. 1 Pet. 3:1–2.

37. Gen. 12:1–8; 12:10–20; 20:1–18.
38. Acts 5:29.
39. 1 Pet. 2:18–20; see also Matt. 5:44–45.
40. 1 Pet. 3:6.
41. See Esther 5:2–8.
42. Acts 4:29–31.
43. Josh. 6:17, 22–25.
44. Matt. 1:5.
45. 1 Sam. 25:23–35.
46. 1 Sam. 25:39–42.
47. Esther 2:9, 15, 17, 20; 5:2; 4:14, 16.
48. Esther 2:20.
49. Esther 2:8–9, 15.
50. Esther 2:17; 5:2–4; 8:3.
51. Esther 4:14–16.
52. Esther 5:2–4; 7:3; 8:3–8.
53. Col. 1:27.
54. Matt. 5:17–20.
55. Matt. 22:37–40; John 13:34; Eph. 4:24–32; 1 John 2:8; 3:23.
56. Rom. 12:2; 2 Cor. 4:16; 5:17; Eph. 4:24; Col. 3:10.
57. Num. 12:3; Heb. 11:24–26.
58. Henry Drummond, *The Greatest Thing in the World* (Old Tappan, N.J.: Fleming H. Revell Company, n.d.), 33.
59. Rom. 1:7.
60. Matt. 5:13–16.
61. James 1:21–24.
62. 2 Tim. 2:13.
63. 2 Tim. 1:12.
64. Isa. 43:2–3.
65. Rev. 21:4.
66. Rom. 8:37–39; 1 Pet. 5:10.
67. Matt. 5:14–16; Rom. 8:29–30.
68. Ps. 126:5–6.
69. Deut. 4:1; 16:20.
70. Isa. 61:7.
71. Ps. 37:16; Prov. 15:16.
72. Rom. 8:17; 1 Pet. 3:7.
73. Phil. 4:11, 13.
74. Prov. 3:5–6.

⚜ 4 ⚜

A Diet That Welcomes Gains

BE SUBMISSIVE:
LET YOUR ATTITUDE BE GOVERNED BY OBEDIENCE

The Context: Matthew 5:3–12

**"Blessed are those who hunger
and thirst for righteousness,
For they shall be filled."**

MATTHEW 5:6

In the first three Beatitudes, the character of the one who has been awakened and filled with the Spirit of God is described. First, she is to realize her own inadequacy and need, being "poor in spirit" and marked by humility. Second, she is conscious of her own sinfulness and guilt and "mourns" over the nothingness and emptiness it brings. Third, she refuses to try to justify herself before the Lord. Instead she allows God to control her life through her meek and gentle spirit.

In the fourth beatitude, which is discussed in this chapter, the perspective changes. The ideas expressed in the earlier Beatitudes may be more difficult to understand, but everyone knows what it means to be hungry and thirsty.[1] The nature of your "hunger and thirst" may appear in various forms, but always it pertains primarily to the basic necessities for living the Christian life.

In Third World countries from Africa to Asia to Europe to South America, I have seen food and water shortages and people suffering from deprivation. But never did I have a more poignant experience than in Uganda. I was there within a few months of the removal of the ruthless dictator Idi Amin. Added to the horrors of ruthless killing and the stench of death was the tragedy of hunger and starvation.

The fertile and productive country identified by Winston Churchill as "the pearl of Africa" had once been noted for its natural resources. But now the nation had been stripped and raped in a tragic way. Fresh vegetables and meat were almost nonexistent. Even rice was scarce. I had to bring a supply of rice from Kenya for our student teams. The water supply had widespread contamination. The children cried for candy, which they called "sweeties." They stuffed their hungry stomachs with what looked like a banana. In reality this "fruit" look-alike had no nutritional value but gave empty stomachs the feeling of being full.

Most of our students experienced dehydration from sieges of vomiting and diarrhea. Our strong athletic son lost more than twenty pounds during the eight weeks he conducted basketball clinics throughout the country. The students, like the people of this barren land, were hungry and thirsty, but they could not eat or drink.

During the time my husband served as chairman of an area committee for the International Mission Board, we traveled with Lewis and Toni Meyers to the countries within the appointed area. One of the countries we visited was the small and, at the time of our visit, newly independent nation of Kazakhstan. Our visit coincided with a special festival, and we were graciously welcomed by government leaders.

One of the most unique experiences during our travel throughout the country was our flight to the Arel Sea. The flight in itself was an experience long to be remembered as we boarded an airplane built before the date of my birth. There was no need to have a device for reclining your seat because the plane's nose pointed upward—higher than its tail—so that we literally sank into our seats, falling into a reclining position. There was no air conditioning, and only one side of the seat belt was attached to each passenger's seat. But the aircraft managed to take off, fly us to our destination, and land us safely!

Once on the ground we were overwhelmed with soaring heat—more than 115°—and dunes of sand lay before us as far as the eye could see. In the midst of the sand dunes were many large ships. Because of tragic mismanagement of resources, the tremendous body of water had disappeared so quickly that huge ships were left stranded. The entire economy was destroyed; water and food became scarce. Without basic sustenance or a means of supplying those needs, these people knew hunger and thirst so acutely that they were driven to find other ways to satisfy their hunger and thirst.

This tragic experience for the people in the region of the Arel Sea became an object lesson for me in the spiritual arena. All the tangibles that I depend upon to sustain me can quickly be lost whether by unfortunate events or wrong choices. However, my hunger and thirst for the things of the Lord must be so basic and consuming that I am

driven to the Lord to get what no one else can give and to receive
what no one else can take away.[2] Such driving passion harnesses my
heart and controls my spirit so that my focus rests upon the Lord
Jesus. My only genuine satisfaction comes from resting in Him. The
path to my resting in Him is personal commitment to do what He says!

A Woman's Wisdom

"Find happiness in your heart, not your happenstance."

—Luci Swindoll

These metaphors of seeking righteousness as the hungry look for
bread and as the thirsty search for water were vivid and powerful. No
person or animal can live without food and water. Each meal satisfies.
The fact that you must eat again does not mean you were not satisfied
by meals previously consumed. It does affirm that you must continue
to take in food and water under the continuing stimulus of your nor-
mal appetite. When appetite wanes, the body signals some problem.

The same is true in the spiritual life. A good appetite indicates health
and vigor and growth (perhaps for some of you, more than you would
like). However, whether in the physical or spiritual realm, what sustains
life is not merely a substance that provides satiation. God has placed in
every human being an insatiable hunger for Himself—what someone has
described as a God-shaped vacuum. What extends life and health spiritually will be found only in the life-giving reservoir of God Himself.[3]

The Lord admonished His children to request "daily bread."[4] You
cannot find answers for tomorrow's spiritual yearnings yesterday or
even today. You must continually hunger and thirst for the sacred food
that the Lord alone can provide. His answ s c e i a quiet, refreshing oasis, and they come day by day. Remember the manna God
provided for the Israelites in the wilderness. It had to be gathered

daily, and each person was responsible for her own needs;[5] but God was faithful![6]

The verb (Greek *chortasthēsontai*) is in the passive voice, i.e., "They shall be filled," which means that the filling is to be done by an outside agent. You are to be the object of the filling, but the Lord Himself will fill you! The verb is also in the future tense, which indicates that the filling is not a one-time event. God means for the feeding and the satisfaction and the growing to continue. The attention is not frozen on the individual and her character but extends to the importance of her relationship with God. This bonding is established through an intense longing for what she realizes is missing and what she urgently needs in her own life.

No woman can have all of God and appropriate all of His righteousness. God intends for you to acquire a perpetual appetite for His righteousness, knowing that He alone can provide spiritual satisfaction.

Satisfaction for the Seeking

Palestine has long been a place marked by hunger and thirst, the strongest and most familiar desires of the physical nature. Life and prosperity depended upon the seasons, and harvests were dependent upon rains and the timing of that precipitation.

On the streets of Jerusalem and other cities in the Middle East, you still hear the cry of the waterseller. One of my prized treasures is an ancient skin bottle from the Beersheva Bedouin Market. An animal skin stitched together, the container held its refreshing liquid for many years before it ended up buried in a dirty marketplace. There I retrieved the vessel, cleaned it, and hung it in our pantry. Every time I pass through and see the skin, I remember the prophet's words, "Ho! everyone who thirsts, Come to the waters." The prophet is careful to include in his extended invitation the idea of satisfaction that is to come for the hungry and thirsty. The people are called to quench their thirst and assuage their hunger.[7]

From infancy, you have known these physical pangs and responded to them in dramatic ways. You can be certain that they will be with you as long as you have life. The infant cries for food even though he does not understand his need. There is simply a vague lack of something.

My adorable granddaughter has a smart mother, as you might suspect. When we are going to a restaurant to eat, even if we leave in time to eat at the hour appointed for Abigail's mealtime, there is always the possibility of extenuating circumstances—long lines of people waiting to be seated, poor service after seating, a mix-up in orders, etc. Just for such exigencies, Abigail's mother always has some snacks in her emergency bag. It is amazing what a few cheerios or a small cracker or a few sips of milk can do to curb the hunger of a child. Unfortunately, most believers have not transferred this helpful principle into their spiritual lives so that they can be refueled and renewed on the run and even during those unexpected moments of need. God has given the resources—the Holy Spirit and the Bible. You only have to appropriate them in a timely way.[8]

In addition to physical hunger and thirst, most people recognize another craving—the craving of the mind for knowledge. Curiosity and an inquisitive mind will drive an individual to seek knowledge at great cost and with much effort.[9]

Far more important than physical and mental hunger and thirst, however, is the spiritual craving of the soul. Though seldom recognized and even less often acknowledged, this longing supersedes all other longings.

When my father had a major heart attack almost two decades ago, he was middle-aged and seemingly in excellent health. He oversaw the operation of his own business in addition to his labors in the community and in his church. He had a premonition about the attack and left his business to go to the doctor's office without an appointment. That choice saved his life since he was in the doctor's office when the most serious attack occurred. He was immediately prepared for open-heart surgery.

Shortly after Dad left the hospital to continue his convalescence at home, we were talking about the changes in lifestyle that must be forthcoming for him. "Dorothy, I've always lived to eat," Dad said. "Now I must eat to live." Dad realized that his physical hunger and thirst must now be channeled in a different way. As important as food is to nourish the body, it is not the main thing—not when living and breathing are on the ballot!

The same is true of knowledge. Knowledge, or simply acquiring a vast collection of facts for its own sake, is of little importance; but when this knowledge is used to serve and to contribute to life, it becomes an important tool. Yes, you eat to live, and you learn to serve. But remember, too, that you live for and serve the living Lord—this is the purpose and mission of every believer!

Naomi's husband, Elimelech, made the decision to take his family away from their ancestral home in Bethlehem and into the pagan land of Moab because there was a "famine" in the land.[10] Since the biblical record makes no mention of Elimelech's being called out of Bethlehem, this decision may have come from his own heart. In any case, the consequences were disastrous. Hunger and thirst are powerful forces that sometimes overwhelm other important factors.

The land of the Bible has been plagued by hunger and thirst across the years, including the present era with the numerous refugees seeking sustenance. Life is a struggle for every generation. Jesus picked up this common plight and applied it to the spiritual realm.

The Priority of Life

Moving directly into a discussion on the priority of life, Jesus used a metaphor to describe intense longing and desire. A follower of Jesus Christ is to "hunger and thirst after righteousness," to long for intimacy with God—a relationship with God that can only be realized by allowing Christ to live in you. In other words, a genuine disciple of Christ will always be dissatisfied with where she is in her discipleship.

What is "righteousness"? Righteousness is that which corresponds to the will of God. Of the seven times Matthew used "righteousness" (Greek *dikaiosunē*), five occur in the Sermon on the Mount.[11] In the Greek text, the article is included (more literally translated "the right-eousness") so that it is the whole of righteousness that is demanded and not just isolated deeds.

Righteousness for some people means morality kept on a socially or religiously acceptable plane. However, God's definition of righteous-ness is living like the Lord Jesus; His standard is the life of Christ. When you realize this awesome challenge, you are suddenly over-whelmed with the task of seeking His righteousness.

One of the first steps in this holy quest is to take a good look at your own false righteousness. You know that certain things in the world are against God and His righteousness. They are harmful and sinful. Too many believers are not willing to avoid blatant sin, much less run from anything that tends to dull the spiritual appetite or pull them away from the Lord. There are also some things that are not bad in themselves. But if left unchecked, they can consume your time and energies so that you do not have time for the things of the Lord. It is the same as filling your stomach with junk food instead of nutritional vegetables.

How about television, radio, movies, catalogs, newspapers, and magazines? Sporting or entertainment events? Computers or other technology? My own life becomes quite cluttered even with good things. When I travel for a lengthy period, I like to have all newspapers and catalogs saved. I figure there might be some worthy news or event that would provide good illustrative material; so I want to go through the mound of papers. Catalogs are a recreational pursuit for me. A month away from Magnolia Hill can bring five hundred catalogs await-ing my return. I decided that I had to clear some clutter from my life.

Before my last extended trip, I asked a staff member to watch the daily newspaper for any noteworthy item I should see and then discard the papers. I ordered all catalogs to be given or thrown away before my return so I would not be tempted to wade through them. What a difference it made just to implement these simple changes.

My son Armour helped me in this area as well. When he moved back to Texas, he left his television set, which he removed from his own room to his father's library. That move was so his parents would be drawn to the treadmill by the enticement of watching television during exercise (a fruitless effort in itself). When I asked about the TV set, Armour said that his books were more important. He commented that there was little on television worth watching. He prefers hiking to watch the sunrise or sunset and enjoying solitude to watching television.

Taping special features on television to watch at a later time used to be important to me. I rationalized that so little good appeared in the programming that I did not want to miss what might be profitable. However, I found it quite time-consuming to set up the recorder, to label what was recorded, and then to find the time to watch the feature. Now I seldom use the recorder. If something I want to see comes at a convenient time, I'll tune in. If not, I'll wait for the rerun or just miss it. Armour actually hit upon a good idea—North Carolina sunsets are great, too!

What a difference would occur in my own life if I were as serious about clearing out spiritual clutter as I am in clearing out mail and papers! How much better to avoid the world's clutter of paper and event to give myself time for clearing spiritual clutter through the most important pursuit—hungering and thirsting for His righteousness. Satisfying spiritual appetites is a time-consuming discipline. It demands ordering your personal life. Spending time reading the Bible and communicating with God must be priorities around which all else revolves. And somehow you must give God the best time—not just what is left after you've done everything else.

Essentially three aspects of "righteousness" must be considered in this sermon in light of the Old Testament usage of the term. "Righteousness" is *soteriological.* It describes a new relationship between God and those who turn to Him in repentance and faith. It is also *ethical* in its demand for a lifestyle of divinely stamped harmonious relationships with others. Finally, it has an *eschatological* or Christological dimension. It expresses the new relationship that the believer will have with God and with others as a result of Jesus' ministry and teachings.

The term may describe spiritual blessings in a cumulative way: "But seek first the kingdom of God and His righteousness, and all these things shall be added to you."[12] There is certainly the essence of salvation included in this word. In Christ is provided a perfect righteousness for all who turn to Him. He alone satisfies the demands of God's holiness. He becomes the atonement for the sins and the substitute to bear the penalty for all who call upon Him. A sinner is justified through the death of Christ when she determines to accept His redemption, thereby becoming legally righteous before God.

The justification found in this "righteousness" is linked to inner sanctification whereby righteousness is not only *imputed* (i.e., in the sense of being legally credited to an account) but also *imparted.* You receive God's favor and find yourself once-and-for-all related to Him, but you also experience a renewing of God's image in you.

The experience operates on two levels. The initial experience comes at the point of conversion with the bestowal of God's grace.[13] What begins at conversion continues in the heart of the believer as she is overwhelmed by a continual desire to eat of the goodness of God that she has tasted.[14] The yearning for salvation by Christ now becomes the longing to be like Him.[15] A closer walk with the Savior focuses your energies on the desire to be conformed more and more to His image.[16] God Himself creates this hunger in the human soul. He fashions it in such a way that only He can satisfy it.[17]

The order is interesting. You would think that the person who is full of righteousness would be blessed. However, the words of Jesus make it clear that the blessed are those who *yearn* for that righteousness—and earnestly so! The blessed have an intense longing for righteousness; they realize that the spiritual journey never ends. Just as you awaken every morning with a fresh appetite for food and water, so your desires for spiritual sustenance should be renewed daily.

Righteousness goes beyond "right doing." "Right doing" is concerned with the bottom line, the results of your deeds. "Righteousness," however, moves to another dimension—your motivation. It must begin with a right relationship to God. This relationship to the Lord is the channel through which your passions are fueled.

There is another interesting lesson to be learned in looking at the importance of righteousness. Your desire for righteousness or rightness with God means that you desire to move away from sinfulness. Sin is not the result of human weakness but the consequence of an individual's disobedience. Consider the prophet Jonah. He did not approve of God's plan for his life, and he thought he could get out of doing things God's way. When God told him to go to Nineveh, he went the opposite direction—to Tarshish.[18] He decided to run from God. I'm sure he planned to do some ministry along the way. However, it is not enough to be willing to do ministry in the Lord's name. Many people, like Jonah, are willing to do certain things in the service of Christ, but they are unwilling to be ready to do anything or go anywhere He directs.

The heart of commitment is more than devotion to service for Christ; it is devotion to *doing* His will. It is being ready to do anything He gives you to do. To put your life completely in His hands is to be willing and determined to do His will. Jonah didn't resign and walk away from his prophetic calling. He felt that he knew better where to exercise his gifts! He was looking for a way to avoid the unpleasant and miss trouble.

What did this prophet find in going his own way? If he had done it God's way, what trouble and heartache he would have missed—being thrown overboard, the traumatic experience of being swallowed by a great fish, coming face-to-face with death, the embarrassment of watching private sin become public correction.[19]

Disobedience is doing what you've been told not to do, and it is costly. When you forget your place in creation, you are acting as if you are God. You are pitting yourself against the Lord Himself. Obedience in God's domain is not mechanical action or mindless slavery. Rather, to be obedient is to understand that blessing and happiness come from obeying the One who is the source of all truth and the essence of all goodness.[20] However, God does not stop with the demand for obedience.

Biblical obedience goes far beyond perfunctory acquiescence to a recognized authority. In fact, it is possible to choose to obey a command outwardly without first giving the inner assent of the heart. In spiritual matters, obedience becomes inwardly the supreme test of genuine faith and outwardly the public testimony of reverence for the Lord. Obedience to the Lord is essential for salvation.[21]

Obedience is also the first step in pleasing God and developing communion with Him because it is the pathway to a set-apart and holy lifestyle. The pathway is long and challenging, but you walk it one step at a time. When you step forward in obedience, the light shines on the next step. Those who follow Christ never walk in darkness. God is most interested in having a set-apart and holy people,[22] and He is willing to walk with you every step of the way. Alone you cannot succeed; but when you do your part, God will do His part.

When you place yourself in God's hands, His life flows through you to accomplish His purposes.[23] God is the sculptor, and you become the chisel with which He is carving His statues. The chisel is a tool for producing the artistry of a statue, but the chisel cannot do its work independently. Just as the sculptor uses the chisel, you can put yourself into the hands of the living Lord to produce something beautiful. Your hands then become His channel for touching the lives of other women.

A Woman's Wisdom

"I vow obedience to You because Your fatherly charity allures me, Your loving kindness and gentleness attract me. In observing Your will, I tie myself to you because clinging to you is lovable above everything."

—St. Gertrude the Great

Joy Cullen, my missionary friend and soul mate, once shared with me a heartrending experience that happened with her youngest daughter Cathy while they were living in Sri Lanka. Joy was visiting Jane and John, her two older children in boarding school in Thailand. Two-year-old Cathy pulled a pan full of frying chicken off the stove. The hot grease splashed over her small body. Though her sister Julie had never been instructed on how to deal with burns, she instinctively grabbed ice and applied it to the burns. There was no resident plastic surgeon in Sri Lanka, but God's providence had an experienced plastic surgeon in the country on that very day to care for another patient. He agreed to administer emergency care to Cathy as well.

Joy returned home to a season of anguish as she had to change Cathy's bandages every day during the slow and agonizing healing process. God was gracious and the burns did heal, but scars would remain to remind Cathy and the entire family of this tragedy. When Cathy was five years old, she asked her mother, "Why did God let that grease burn me?"

Her mother had a wise response: "You were burned by the grease because of your disobedience. Your mommy had warned you about the stove, and your daddy had told you not to get near the chicken, but you reached up to the stove to get that chicken, and you pulled the hot grease over on yourself. Your pain and suffering were the result of your own disobedience."

How often we behave just like Cathy! We know the demands of the Christian life. The Scripture is clear on what God expects of His children. Obedience is surely the most challenging aspect of the Christian life. Yet we become impatient; we see something we want; we become impatient with God's timing. We bring upon ourselves the painful consequences of disobedience.

Of course, obedience is never easy. It often means waiting in the midst of chaos and fear. You don't always understand God's plan for your life, and it is hard to rest in the knowledge that He always has your best interest at heart.[24] You must also understand that you cannot control your conduct in your own strength. Self-discipline or self-control in the spiritual realm is definitely a misnomer. Ultimately the only way to obedience is to place your entire being under the control of Christ. All of your life—whether spiritual, physical, or moral—must be under the management of the Holy Spirit.

You must be a "woman under authority" whose rights have been relinquished and whose will has been placed under the mandate of the heavenly Father.[25] Such commitment precludes going your own way, carving out your own vocational pursuits, doing your own thing, bowing to your own self-determination. You must put aside your own self-rule and turn over the governance of your life to the Lord God.

Amazingly, when you take the risks that accompany obedience, you will find the solid rock of God's faithfulness beneath you.[26] You will also find markers along the way, indicating that others have gone before you.[27] There is no satisfaction like reaping the rewards of obedience.[28]

In this sermon Jesus described the lilies as growing without toil or care from themselves. In fact, the lilies can grow nowhere except where they are planted. Yet they always add radiant beauty to the fields where they are found. You also have the option to bloom where God has planted you, but you can do so only if you sink your roots where He has placed you. If you obey His Word, He will take care of everything else.[29]

In fact, all you are expected to do is to take the first step. He promises to lead you the rest of the way.[30] You must first do what you know before He takes you to the next level in revealing Himself more fully. The only route to truly knowing God is obedience.[31] Obedience is action; God gives you something to do. Your doing what He gives you to do—a single step taken—prepares the way for more light and the next step.

Abraham had to be willing to offer Isaac before he understood how God would circumvent the sacrifice of His Son and then use Abraham's testimony as a picture of God's plan for the redemption of mankind.[32]

A Woman's Wisdom

"Freedom . . . begins not with doing what you want but with doing what you ought."

—Elisabeth Elliot

When you desire to go God's way, you simultaneously determine not to go your own way.[33] Whatever plans you may have, you must be willing to put them aside and allow God's plan to take precedence. This option dictates that you not only long for righteousness but that you also abhor sin. The genuineness of your hungering and thirsting after righteousness will be readily apparent by how you are willing to satisfy these intense cravings. There is a reaching out in dependence to the one who can supply what is needed. Then comes the responsibility to respond to the craving and accept what is given to satisfy that longing. The mingling of dependence and responsibility will result in disciplined obedience.

Obedience means specific action—not just longing, dreaming, thinking, but *doing*. It will be as if you are taken over, called out, acted upon, even possessed by the Spirit of God! When God speaks to you, you will respond. The question then becomes, *How will you respond.* Will you say yes and amen and thus fulfill the Creator's purpose and plan for your life? Or will you say no, not now, someday?

God gave you the option to obey or disobey. Obedience to God is always possible. You can choose whether to go God's way or to pursue your own feelings and desires. Jesus Himself waged a battle between the response of His human nature to death on the cross and His determination to do the will of the Father.[34]

Your feelings, your thoughts, your way of doing something is usually diametrically opposed to God's plan, His thoughts, His way of doing the same thing.[35] You cannot depend upon what you feel like doing to be the same as what you ought to do, as the apostle Paul himself testified.[36] The apostle was not only honest enough to admit his own feelings and failures, but he was also determined to conquer them in the power of the Lord.[37]

The fourth beatitude presupposes spiritual sensitivity. Mary the mother of Jesus expressed the fulfillment of those people who "hunger and thirst after righteousness." She said of these God-seekers, "He has filled the hungry with good things."[38] And Mary herself satisfied her heart's longing by responding to the Lord in humble obedience, "I am the Lord's servant, and I am willing to do whatever he wants."[39]

A woman who has this spiritual trait will have an insatiable desire to hear from the Lord, which is expressed in this beatitude with the metaphor of "hunger" and "thirst." She will also be marked with a determination to do—to respond with obedience or acts of "righteousness." In the Old Testament, obedience suggests an active response to what you hear rather than passive listening.[40] Who would acknowledge hearing a word from God and yet refuse to act on that word?[41]

Obedience in the New Testament comes from a Greek root (*hupoakouo,* literally "to hear under"), which clearly implies not only a hearing but also the intent to do what you are asked to do.[42] More often than not you operate out of a sense of duty in your life and work, and duties can be explained. However, what you do for the Lord is not duty to be understood and explained. Rather, doing what God says to do is cut-and-dried obedience—no explanation necessary![43]

Trust and Obey

When we walk with the Lord
In the light of his Word
What a glory he sheds on our way!
Let us do his good will;
He abides with us still,
And with all who will trust and obey.
But we never can prove
The delights of his love
Until all on the altar we lay;
For the favor he shows
And the joy he bestows
Are for them who will trust and obey.

Then in fellowship sweet
We will sit at his feet
Or we'll walk by his side in the way;
What he says we will do,
When he sends we will go;
Never fear, only trust and obey.

Trust and obey, for there's no other way
To be happy in Jesus,
But to trust and obey.[44]

Obedience is linked with hearing and believing. This spiritual discipline is a reflection of the love you have for Christ and your commitment to Him. You hear God's command; you believe that it is true; you assume the responsibility to obey the heavenly mandate. Obedience is not a natural response; in fact, it is the antithesis of what is natural (i.e., to go your own way). Obedience flows out of love.[45] You learn obedience; but before you learn, you commit yourself to "hear under" in the same sense that you listen for divine instruction with an inner commitment to do what the Lord says.

A Woman's Wisdom

"Never be obstinate, especially in things of no moment. Christ does not force our will, He only takes what we give Him. But He does not give Himself entirely until He sees that we yield ourselves entirely to Him."

—St. Teresa of Avila

My husband and I have made many trips to Israel. We love the Galilee region and never miss the opportunity to go out on the Sea of Galilee. Many sites have been declared holy just because Helena, the mother of the Emperor Constantine, declared them to be so during her spiritual pilgrimage to Jerusalem in the fourth century.[46] These sites hold little significance to me. However, there are some geographical points—like the beautiful Sea of Galilee—that are authentic. This place draws me to its shores and the beautiful waters.

When the sailboat pushes away from shore, the vessel has the freedom to move swiftly and gracefully through the waters empowered by the winds. On the other hand, storms can quickly descend to disturb even the calmest waters. When the storms come, the boat's experienced crew members know that the boat must forfeit its freedom and yield to the patrol boat, which will tow the sailboat to its safe harbor. The sailboat has not lost the potential strength of its sails that so effectively harness the wind and move the boat on the open sea. However, it is the willingness of the boat to harness its strength when the storms come that provides safe towing to the shore.

Jesus illustrated this principle in His own life when He chose to humble Himself before the Father, not because of weakness but because of strength. He chose to submit His own will to the will of the Father.[47]

A Word of Wisdom

God said it; that settles it; it doesn't matter whether I believe it!

The evidences of such overwhelming desire are apparent. The Holy Spirit begins the stirring of the heart; He reveals His perfect standard; then you must acknowledge your own inability to measure up to that standard in your own strength; the inevitable result is the "hunger and thirst" generated by the Holy Spirit to cause you to look outside yourself for answers.

The Discipline of Discontent

An interesting account of treasure hunter Mel Fisher came across my desk. Fisher spent fourteen years searching for sunken treasure. He lived and breathed with a driving passion to find treasures. Finally, he found the great treasure. Then after an initial spontaneous burst of joy over the accomplishment of his goal, the satisfaction of his hunger and thirst for the affluence and recognition that would come from such a feat, he suddenly felt empty and depressed. He immediately started another search.

Many women are just like this treasure hunter, striving to obtain more and more things to enhance their lives. However, like Mel Fisher, in the final analysis they don't find the satisfaction with "things" to be lasting.

A Woman's Wisdom

"Just as Jesus found it necessary to sweep the money-changers from the Temple porch, so we ourselves need a lot of housecleaning."

—Dale Evans Rogers

Happiness is often defined as freedom from all distress on one hand and the abundance of pleasure on the other. Of course, the Judeo-Christian ethic holds that God created mankind for a purpose. To be made "in the image of God" would be unimportant if life consisted only in the pursuit of happiness and contentment.

My granddogs can slip into nirvana with some simple pleasures—being with me in a hot and crowded car instead of being put in a plush air-conditioned room alone, being served a spoon of plain yogurt rather than a bowl of dog food, or being able to sniff the surroundings of a new walking route on a leash instead of being free to run in a large fenced yard at the kennel. A dog at the feet of her mistress, a cat curled up in front of the family fireplace, a cow in the midst of a green pasture—these are pictures of contentment far beyond what most human beings enjoy.

The hedonist seeks to gratify his physical desires, and he may find momentary contentment in this. But those physical desires may change by the moment or be affected by the circumstances. On the other hand, real meaning in life lies in the spiritual realm. To seek this deepest meaning is to "hunger and thirst after righteousness," to be governed by a unique spiritual sensitivity.

During a visit to Switzerland, Paige and I drove over the border to the German community of Constance on the Lake. We had only a short time but decided to skip lunch and an afternoon nap to visit some of the sites associated with the fifteenth-century Anabaptist John Hus. In

1415 he was martyred because he refused to recant his commitment to believer's baptism. A small museum has been established to honor the life of this courageous Czech preacher of the gospel. On its walls in the entryway are these penetrating words [a rough translation given to me by the curator] from Hus:

"Search for the truth;
Learn the truth to understand the truth;
Love the truth."

Isn't this the essence of hungering and thirsting after righteousness? Hus sealed his obedience with a willingness to lay down his life in the flames of death. He had searched for God and learned the truth (i.e., he was filled with righteousness). Then he was possessed by God's grace, which enabled him to obey God and die for the faith.

You will probably never be called to martyrdom for your faith, but your challenge is the same as that faced by John Hus: You must hunger and thirst for the truth. When you do, you will learn; when you learn, you will love!

Mary of Bethany was a woman with an appetite for spiritual things. Seemingly, Mary was single, living with her sister Martha and brother Lazarus. They were close to Jesus, friends who apparently offered their home to the Lord as a retreat for rest and relaxation. These young adults evidently enjoyed fellowship with one another.

The greatest testimony of Mary's life is her announced desire to sit at Jesus' feet. She did indeed "hunger and thirst after righteousness."[48] She is also identified by many as the woman who anointed Jesus with the costly ointment.[49] The scene occurred in Simon's house in Bethany, a small village separated from Jerusalem only by a valley and the community in which Mary lived. Jesus had been invited to supper. Women would not have been among the invited guests, but they may have been present as hostesses to the group.

Nevertheless, Mary entered the room and approached Jesus. Keep in mind that in the house of a leper, touching would have been forbidden under any circumstances. Yet Mary had a mission to which she was committed. She did not speak but let her actions express her heart. She proceeded to break an elegant and precious alabaster flask and to let its fragrant contents (which consisted of an oil even more valuable than its container) fall upon the head of the Savior. In the Gospel of Mark, the oil is valued at 300 denarii.[50] Since 25 denarii equaled a day's wage, this was a sacrificial gift. Mary was absorbed in her act of worship. She presented to Jesus all that she had.[51]

What a wonderful testimony to pass on to women of every generation: Do what you can where you are with what you have while you can. This woman expressed her love for the Savior in an extravagant and sacrificial way.

A Woman's Wisdom

"When I eat or drink, move or stand still, speak or keep silent, sleep or wake, see, hear, or think; whether I am in church, at home, or in the street, in bad health or good, dying or not dying, at every hour and moment of my life I wish all to be in God. I wish to be unable to wish or do or think or speak anything that is not completely God's will; and the part of me which would oppose this I would wish to be turned into dust and scattered in the wind."

—St. Catherine of Genoa

Mary of Bethany was not looking just to take in whatever the Savior offered, but she also determined to give out to Him whatever she had of value. Not much is said about the words of Mary; rather, she acted out her heart commitment. Her spiritual desires were rewarded as the Savior spent time teaching her spiritual truths and encouraging her in the pursuit of holiness of life.

A Woman's Wisdom

"Christ himself came down and took possession of me. . . . I had never foreseen the possibility of that, of a real contact, person to person, here below, between a human being and God . . . in this sudden possession of me by Christ, neither my sense nor my imagination had any part: I only felt in the midst of my suffering the presence of a love."

—Simone Weil

I interviewed the actress Jeanette Clift George after her filming of *The Hiding Place,* the movie based on the life of Corrie ten Boom. I asked Jeanette to describe Corrie in one word. She answered immediately, "Obedience!"

Greatly admired for her steadfastness in the midst of persecution and suffering, Corrie herself always pointed to the Lord's faithfulness in leading her. To be a committed follower, you must be obedient to the one who is leading. This attitude draws the line between personal rights and divine mandates; it underscores the difference between innate freedoms under the umbrella of divine providence and unbridled license that is seized according to personal desires. You can be obedient by choosing to act with your will even though you do not understand the why or may not want to comply with the mandate issued.

A Woman's Wisdom

"The mind of a Christian should be always composed, temperate, free from all extremes of mirth or sadness, and always disposed to hear the voice of God's Holy Spirit."

—Susanna Wesley

In the Book of Revelation, there are familiar words of petition: "And the Spirit and the bride say, 'Come!' And let him who hears say, 'Come!' And let him who thirsts come. Whoever desires, let him take the water of life freely."[52] Jesus is echoing the invitation of the Holy Spirit and the church. This is a natural response from the Holy Spirit. He has the assignment to reveal things to come[53] and to glorify the Son[54] as well as to motivate the church to a constant yearning for the fulfillment of the events precipitating the return of Christ. This invitation ties in with the beatitude discussed in this chapter as the invitation invites the one who is thirsty to "come." The thirsty one receives an invitation from Christ.

The thirst is spiritual in nature.[55] It is a thirst for the water of life.[56] Note the clarification describing this thirsty person as one who "desires"—anyone who is conscious of a desire for life on a higher plane. The use of "whoever" suggests that the individual with a spiritual hunger may not realize that she is thirsty, but the "desire" for spiritual food may lead her to a search that is so earnest that she actually feels "thirsty."[57] The spiritual provision is free for the taking and thus the gracious invitation. But there is a constant tension between the divine provision of grace and the human responsibility to accept this invitation in obedience. The filling of the heart with spiritual food follows the appetite that arouses the senses to realize the need for this spiritual provision.

A Woman's Wisdom

Let nothing disturb thee,
Let nothing affright thee.
All things are passing.
God never changes.
Patience gains all things.
Who has God wants nothing.
God alone suffices.

—St. Theresa of Avila

For a woman to surrender herself to the Lord in obedience to His Word and in pursuit of His way is not natural or easy. But it is the only way to find genuine happiness and to experience the greatest blessings of God.

When Jesus surrendered Himself to the Father, He modeled ultimate obedience by laying down His life.[58] But that emptying of Himself was not the end, for He arose from the dead. Through His resurrection, He became a living example that blessings are inevitably the fruit of obedience.[59] However, total surrender is not possible without really knowing who God is (the Creator and Ruler of the universe) and understanding what He says (reading His message to you in the Bible). Then you are ready to commit yourself to do what He says because of who He is.[60] And that is when the blessings come!

Prayer and Meditation

Lord, I do hunger and thirst for knowledge of you and for an understanding of Your Word. To know You is to love You; to love You is to want to be like You; to be like You is to pour myself out in service to You; to serve You is to obey Your commands.

With the psalmist, I pour out my heart and echo the passionate call for sustenance and filling, yearning for Your presence in the midst of my own pressures and sorrows: "As the deer pants for the water brooks, so pants my soul for You, O God. My soul thirsts for God, for the living God."[61]

Moments for Enrichment

A VERSE TO MEMORIZE

> Trust in the Lord with all your heart,
> And lean not on your own understanding;
> In all your ways acknowledge Him,
> And He shall direct your paths (Prov. 3:5–6).

ACTIVITIES TO ENHANCE YOUR UNDERSTANDING OF THE TEXT

1. Explore the concept of "famine" in your own spiritual life by considering the desires of your heart for spiritual food.
2. Look closely at Psalm 119 to consider effective ways to seek a Word from God.

Biblical Principle	Reference	Life Application

3. Consider how the concept of righteousness is used in Scripture— as an attribute of God and as a characteristic of believers.
4. Review your own requirements for spiritual nourishment. Prepare a plan for personal spiritual growth—your own way of sitting at the feet of the Master.

Notes

1. Ps. 143:6.
2. Ps. 84:2.
3. Ps. 63:1–2.
4. Matt. 6:11.
5. Exod. 16:21.
6. Exod. 16:15.
7. Isa. 55:1–2.
8. John 14:16; Ps. 119:9–16.
9. Eccl. 12:12.
10. Ruth 1:1–2.
11. Matt. 3:15; 5:6, 10, 20; 6:1, 33; 21:32.
12. Matt. 6:33.
13. Eph. 2:8.
14. Ps. 42:1.
15. Phil. 3:8–14.
16. Rom. 12:1–2; 1 John 3:2.
17. Rev. 7:16.
18. Jon. 1:1–3.
19. See Jon. 1:10–17.
20. John 14:6; see also Ps. 34:8; 136:1.
21. Heb. 5:9.
22. 1 Sam. 15:22.
23. Gal. 2:20.
24. See Ps. 37:7; 46:10; Isa. 30:21.
25. Phil. 3:7–14.
26. Lam. 3:22–25.
27. Deut. 30:19–20; 31:3, 8.
28. Exod. 15:26.
29. Matt. 6:28–30.
30. Prov. 3:5–6; see also 1 Cor. 10:13.
31. 1 John 2:3.
32. See Gen. 22:1–14.
33. Prov. 3:5–6.
34. Matt. 26:39.
35. Isa. 55:8–9.
36. Rom. 7:15–20.

37. Phil. 3:13; 4:13.
38. Luke 1:53.
39. Luke 1:38 Living Bible.
40. See Exod. 24:7; Deut. 21:18–21.
41. Exod. 19:5.
42. Eph. 6:1; Phil. 2:12.
43. 1 John 5:3.
44. John H. Sammis, "When We Walk with the Lord," 1887.
45. 1 John 2:3–4.
46. A.D. 326.
47. Phil. 2:5–8; see also Ps. 40:8; Heb. 10:7.
48. Luke 10:39; John 11:32; 12:3.
49. Matt. 26:6–13; Mark 14:1–9; John 11:1–6.
50. Mark 14:5.
51. Mark 14:8.
52. Rev. 22:17.
53. John 16:13.
54. John 16:14.
55. Matt. 5:6; Rev. 7:16; John 6:35; 7:37.
56. Rev. 21:6; 22:1; see also Isa. 55:1.
57. Jer. 29:13; Mark 7:6.
58. Phil. 2:5–8.
59. Phil. 2:9–11.
60. James 1:22–25.
61. Ps. 42:1–2a.

⁜ 5 ⁜

The Sweetest of All Gifts

BE COMPASSIONATE:
A PASSION FOR GOD MEANS COMPASSION
FOR OTHERS

The Context: Matthew 5:3–12

**"Blessed are the merciful,
For they shall obtain mercy."**

MATTHEW 5:7

Some people would say that this is the most arresting of the Beatitudes. The direction moves beyond your own character to focus on how you relate to others. Those who show "mercy" are rare indeed. Being merciful involves the outworking of your faith—not a faith that *contains* works but one that *pursues* works so they are the outworking of a personal faith. Though each beatitude brings conviction to the sensitive heart, the call to mercy must be a constant reminder of deeds you have done and those you would leave undone.

Mercy is more than a feeling; it is a deep-seated principle for responding to need. Not only is the heart of a woman who extends mercy stirred within, but her entire being is moved to help the person in need. Mercy does not issue forth only in carefully chosen words, but it will be accompanied by helpful acts. To have mercy is to exhibit a gracious spirit of kindness toward others, especially those who are afflicted with sufferings.

Elizabeth, the wife of Zacharias and mother of John the Baptist, was not only a woman of integrity and obedience,[1] but she was also a woman who extended mercy. She faced her own challenges in the physical and emotional changes of a late-life pregnancy and perhaps even curiosity or ridicule from friends because of her condition. Yet she looked beyond herself to see Mary, the humble maiden who happened to be her young, and perhaps distant, cousin. Without sitting in judgment on the younger woman who found herself in an embarrassing situation that could not be explained to the satisfaction of human reasoning, Elizabeth took Mary into her own home and became her mentor and friend.

No mention is made of Mary's own mother, who may have been indifferent to her daughter's situation or perhaps even deceased. Elizabeth became the spiritual mother who stepped in to encourage and prepare Mary for her role as the mother of Messiah. Elizabeth dispensed a large dose of mercy; but she also experienced divine mercy

as she in her old age, having been childless, became the mother of the
Messiah's forerunner.

Revenge for wrongdoing is not an option for a person who is merciful. Even the administration of justice is tempered with mercy, and
retaliation is not in the picture. Miriam, the respected leader of the
women of Israel, was a woman who received mercy. She was not only a
gifted leader but also a poet, musician, and prophetess.[2] She had been
an integral part of Moses' leadership team. He had respected her and
also depended upon her. Perhaps Miriam resented the encroachment
of another woman into the family circle.

For whatever reasons, Miriam allowed her jealousy toward her
brother's wife to open her heart to bitterness, which manifested itself
in murmuring and even in her blatant rejection of Moses' leadership.
However, Moses responded with mercy toward Miriam even after she
had rebelled against him and the Lord. When the Lord administered
severe punishment to Miriam in the form of leprosy, Moses interceded
on her behalf and cried out to the Lord to heal his sister.[3]

We dare not look smugly at Miriam, judging her bitterness and
rebellion. Who has not made a hasty judgment of a spouse, friend, or
neighbor? What woman has not sharply criticized her husband or child
or friend? Who has not been so absorbed in her own world that she
has been insensitive to another's pain or sorrow? Jealous, spiteful, dis-
obedient, Miriam needed and received mercy.

In contrast to Miriam, who needed mercy, are Shiprah and Puah,
two other women who were her contemporaries. These women served
as midwives in Egypt, evidently giving special attention to helping
women in the Hebrew community give birth to their children. These
women feared God more than they feared Pharaoh,[4] and they refused
to destroy the male babies but rather saved them alive. Among those
who experienced their mercies was Moses, the great leader of Israel.
As a result of their courage and mercy, these women were blessed of
God,[5] and their names are recorded in Scripture for the generations

(note that the name of the pharaoh is not recorded). God extended His mercies to Shiprah and Puah and through them to others.

This beatitude calling for the ministry of compassion follows in logical sequence. The truths found in these Beatitudes serve as a searchlight into your innermost soul and as a scalpel to cut through even the hardest heart. The arresting light and painful cutting are essential as a means of mirroring to you who you are and how you measure up to God's pattern for the Christian lifestyle.

Once you see yourself as you are before the Lord, you cannot help but be humbled to the point of extending your compassions to others. You are irresistibly drawn to those who are sick, those who are hurting from injustices, those who are wretched and rejected. The merciful are not receiving what they lack, but they are getting more of what they already have and are using. They have mercy and show mercy, and thus they will experience mercy.

Remember the publican (tax collector) who humbly prayed, "God, be merciful to me a sinner."[6] In contrast to the Pharisee—who seemed more interested in the earthly audience who might hear him than in the heavenly Father to whom he prayed—the publican bowed before the Lord, beating his breast as a sign of his overwhelming grief. God heard the prayer of the humble publican. He commended him, rather than the outwardly religious Pharisee, as being "justified."

A Woman's Wisdom

Near the cross, a trembling soul,
Love and mercy found me;
There the bright and Morning Star
Sheds its beams around me.

—Fanny J. Crosby,
"Jesus, Keep Me Near the Cross"

Distribution from Abundance

Equipping yourself to be merciful is not a condition of emptiness for God to fill but is the result of what has already been experienced as God's provision. Having and giving out mercy assumes the possession of righteousness. For example, a lifeguard trying to save a drowning woman must first be safe from going under herself. Only then can she pull her sister from the waters. The sense of meaning found in "merciful" (Greek *eleēmones*) is more than feeling. Rather, it connotes conscious and compassionate action. To be merciful requires human initiative spawned by unconditional love.

Scripture describes two kinds of mercy and grace. The Lord Jesus gives you His unmerited mercy when in your helpless and sinful condition you go to Him in faith; then comes the merited mercy of God because of your acts of mercy to others. God's dividends are amazing. Mercy administered by a believer is an outgrowth of her relationship to God; she is demonstrating and using what she has received.

Mercy is not simply pity, nor is it merely emotion. To extend mercy is to act with the will; it is to share the experience of another and in so doing to act in that person's behalf.[7] The more mercy you extend to others, the more mercy you receive from God. Personal helplessness draws divine mercy; and once extended, mercifulness attracts more mercy.

The "law of liberty" mentioned in James 2:13 is actually the law of God's liberality or mercy. Mercy does not dismiss sin and its consequences. Mercy does not bypass or cancel out justice but rather is founded upon perfect justice so that any believer who does not show mercy to others will not receive the Father's mercy.[8]

The amount of mercy believers experience in heaven will be proportionate to the amount of mercy they have shown while on earth.[9] Just as you need to be saved in order to share that salvation effectively with someone else, you cannot truly show mercy unless you have first experienced it; you cannot give what you do not have. In God's economy, she who gives will always receive more than she gives since God's outpouring is always bigger than ours.

The principle that you cannot outgive God is one that has been proven again and again. There is an inner benefit to the merciful, issuing forth in personal satisfaction.[10] When God is in control of the life of a believer, He makes her God-sufficient. To believe that God is sufficient puts all circumstances in proper perspective. To believe that God is sufficient makes faith the path to blessedness.

A Woman's Wisdom

Lord, you are my lover,
My longing,
My flowing stream,
My sun,
And I am your reflection.

—Mechthild of Magdeburg

To be merciful is not a natural human response, nor is it an inevitable accompaniment to righteous living. The religious leaders of Jesus' day maintained strict standards of righteousness and devoted religious service; yet they sometimes were indifferent to the sufferings of others and without compassion for those who were hurting.[11] The influence of Christianity is indelibly stamped upon relief ministries. Whether or not the actual ministration of tender loving care is done by Christians themselves or by them through a purely secular organization, inevitably the influence of Christianity is there. This is how it should be. Nowhere should tender compassions and selfless service be more apparent than in the church of the living Lord.[12]

The concept of "mercy" is one of the unique paradoxes in Scripture. The word itself seems to rule out the idea of "merit." To be rewarded according to merit is to be paid or rewarded for what you have accomplished. Fortunately, God has never locked Himself into giving you only what you deserve. After you have been bathed in the Lord's undeserved mercy, He proceeds to bestow on you the just rewards of your labor for His name's sake. Even these rewards are not distributed according to the rigid guidelines of a legalistic paymaster but with the generosity of a loving heavenly Father.

Whatever the Lord elects to do for His own is always far greater than what they deserve. Thus, mercy is the divine characteristic that overshadows all other attributes. When God's justice had to be satisfied, He provided a way to do so through the sacrifice of His Son—and that way was through divine mercy.

More Than Tears

Tears often accompany the outpouring of mercy, just as Jesus wept when He felt the loss of His friend Lazarus and saw the grief of Mary and Martha over the death of their brother.[13] But He did not stop with weeping over the death of Lazarus; He immediately showed concern for the grieving family and for the testimony that could come out of this sorrowful experience.

To weep easily is nothing more than an emotional response. Tears can be empty and meaningless except to inspire the use of a Kleenex or handkerchief or to require a redoing of makeup. Even acts of benevolence—working in a soup kitchen, passing out clothing at the rescue mission, volunteering at the pregnancy crisis center—can be done out of duty and without the motivation of a truly merciful heart.

For almost two decades, my husband and I have followed closely the ministry of Armitage Baptist Church, located in the inner city of Chicago. When we first met Charles and Georgia Lyons, we were overwhelmed with their vision to present the mercies of the gospel of Jesus Christ through planting a strong church in the heart of Chicago. We were also impressed with their gift for extending mercy in mundane ways to the people in that great metropolitan area. They began to move toward their goal by finding an abandoned Masonic temple that had been turned into a bingo parlor in one of the crime-ridden, inner-city areas in Chicago. They envisioned this decaying building as a potential lighthouse for the gospel. We had the privilege of joining them in a prayer walk around that seemingly useless building.

Many years later, just as I was completing this manuscript, my husband and I again found ourselves at Armitage. What a difference God had wrought! The building had been purchased, reclaimed, and beautifully refurbished. In fact, the ladies' powder room must be among the most elegant and lovely in Chicago. The room is spotlessly clean; there are ample stalls and sinks; seat covers and paper and full soap dispensers are readily available; a baby changing table is strategically placed; there is a covered can for waste. Nothing is missing in this unique "comfort station"; yet the upper echelons of society may never enter its doors.

To the outsider, it would seem that the character of the church has changed because of the overwhelming cosmetic changes. However, those of us who have followed the church across the years know that the character of the church and its vision have never changed. The pastor and people have been blessed of God with His mercies because they have consistently administered mercy to others.

A look at their current bulletin confirms that they have the same sensitive heart for reaching out to those in need that prompted the church's vision in previous years. They provide transportation for people to and from church worship services; they offer food and clothing assistance through Chicago Hope; they provide substance abuse counseling; they operate support groups such as Hope for Moms for mothers of preschoolers; they are creating extensive ministries for children and youth. The church has complete ethnic diversity within their membership and among the visitors who attend. They have supported sanctity of life, but they also reach out to those whose lives have been marred by abortion. They have opposed homosexuality activism, but homosexuals are welcome to attend their services and hear the gospel. This congregation has certainly been blessed of God, but the rest of the story is that they are also blessing others through extending their mercies to all within their reach.

The emphasis in Christianity has always been upon *being* rather than *doing*. Your attitude will overshadow your actions. Who you are in Christ is more important than what you do in His name! A woman must *be* something (i.e., a genuine believer) before she can *do* anything significant in Jesus' name, like flesh out the Christian lifestyle.

No woman consistently acts like a Christian unless a spiritual transformation has taken place in her own heart. Christianity is not like a ball of modeling clay to be fashioned into an accessory for the life you want to live. You don't control your Christianity; your Christianity must control you. Christianity is not a system for you to use; the Beatitudes are not teachings for you to manipulate. Rather, the Beatitudes are a standard for living the life that Christ challenged His followers to live.

In the beautiful descriptive passage about the "woman of strength" in Proverbs 31, the section begins with a description of the woman's character before it discusses all the things she does in her home and community. This woman begins with the right priorities—nourishing her personal relationship with the Lord and building in her own life humility, integrity, trustworthiness, and commitment to her family. Then she is ready to extend her mercies beyond the family circle. What you *do* is simply the outworking of who you *are*.[14]

A Woman's Wisdom

"My mother, all de time she'd be prayin' to de Lord. She'd take us chillun to de woods to pick up firewood, and we'd turn around to see her down on her knees behind a stump, a-prayin'. We'd see her wipin' her eyes wid de corner of her apron—first one eye, den de other—as we come along back. Den, back in de house, down on her knees, she'd be a-prayin'."

—Rebecca Grant

Genuine mercifulness belongs to the heart. This inner disposition of the soul manifests itself in a forgiving spirit, a compassionate heart, a vision marked by sensitivity, and a patient attitude even with those who have made themselves your enemies.

When spring comes to North Carolina, a living parade of divine handiwork begins. Leaves appear on the trees; the pear trees start to bud; the dogwood comes to life; the azaleas and roses and a host of other flowers bud and bloom; the fragrance of magnolias fills the air. The birds begin to announce the dawn. Our family moves out to the side porch for mealtime. The rabbits begin to play on the lawn. Everyone knows that spring has arrived, not because of what the calendar announces but because of what they can see, smell, and touch all around them!

In the same way, there will be ample evidence that mercy has been enthroned in a woman's heart. A merciful woman will see the best instead of the worst in others; she will be slow to condemn and quick to commend those around her; she will not perform deeds out of perfunctory duty but will lovingly serve those whom the Lord places in her path. She will stoop to get under the load of the person carrying a burden. She

will not be looking for all she can take from the world, but she will open
her heart and hearth to welcome all people, pouring out genuine and loving hospitality. She will have a forgiving spirit, refusing to be embittered
toward those who may have wronged her or her family. She doesn't need
to announce her merciful spirit; it will permeate everything she does.

The Might of the Merciful

God's mercy to you is not conditioned on whether you are merciful
to others. Divine forgiveness is not prompted by human merit but is
the response of a loving Father. However, any woman who has been
the recipient of divine mercy will be compelled to respond in like manner in her own relationships. She will quickly realize that in many
cases the faults she sees and condemns in others are the very ones of
which she herself is guilty.[15]

Jesus used a parable (a simple story with a profound life lesson)
to illustrate this poignant truth. He introduced a prosperous man who
had to confront the steward in charge of his vast estate because of dis-
honesty in the handling of the estate. When the guilty man was called
to give an account, he had no excuses for his lack of integrity in managing the affairs of his master. Knowing the landowner's just and righteous character, the dishonest steward admitted his wrongdoing,
acknowledged that he deserved punishment, and then simply threw
himself on the mercy of his master. Moved with compassion for the
man and his family, the master forgave the man of his enormous debt,
which the man could not have repaid in a lifetime.

Time passed and the steward quickly forgot the mercy extended
to him by his master. After he had handled his master's estate dishon-
estly and then been forgiven by his master of the enormous debt he
had owed, the steward was found trying to exact payment from one of
his peers for a much smaller debt owed to him. He had seized the
debtor and was sending the man to prison, forgetting the mercy he
himself had received.

A report of the servant's unjust actions came before the estate owner. His righteous indignation prompted him to seize the unjust steward and commit him to prison, where the man would have time to reflect on the meaning of mercy.[16] Obviously, one who had experienced such mercy should have been generous in his own judgment of another. He should have been willing and even eager to forgive the debt owed him, since he himself had experienced such forgiveness.

The Pharisees and scribes fell into this same trap. They were obsessed with their own supposed holiness; yet their attitude toward those who were less fortunate (the poor, the lame, the lepers, the outcasts of society) often reflected scorn and disgust. Remember, for example, the woman caught in adultery who was dragged to Jesus. The religious leaders hoped to entrap Jesus by contrasting His commitment to the Law with the merciful love He seemed to practice in His life and teachings. Jesus responded by clarifying the Law and by giving them a wonderful and insightful treatise on mercy.[17]

On the other hand, don't be deceived into believing that to extend mercy is merely to withhold harsh rebuke. Jesus did not refuse to rebuke this woman whose sin had been made public. He acknowledged her sin; then He stretched out arms of loving concern to her. He not only refused to add to her despair and hurt; He also forgave her and offered her a new purpose for living.

No believer would be able to stand before the Father's judgment except for the presence of the Son as mediator. When it comes to forgiving your shortcomings, Jesus is both generous and just. The Father's tenderness in judgment is the result of His unfailing mercies toward His children.[18]

The unnamed woman who boldly entered the home of Simon the Pharisee went directly to Jesus. She was carrying a beautiful alabaster vase. Alabaster is still an exquisite and unique substance that is greatly treasured. It is described as translucent marble. I have some pieces I have painstakingly collected and lovingly placed in our home. One is an ancient Roman alabaster glass mirror. This exquisite piece dates to Roman times. The other is a small oblong covered box, which I purchased in Egypt some years ago.

One of these pieces of alabaster is centuries old and the other was fashioned in the last two decades. But when held to the light, both are greatly enhanced. They exhibit a delicate pattern and muted color that is quite impressive. However, the treasure borne by this woman who came to Jesus went beyond the unique and extravagant container to include an expensive, precious, fragrant and soothing oil.

The woman washed Jesus' feet with her tears. Then she broke the valuable alabaster vase, pouring its costly oil over the feet of the Master. The self-righteous religious leaders present for this unique act of devotion were incredulous. Simon's thought was to ask why Jesus would even allow such a woman to approach Him. Jesus had an explanation: She loved much because she had been forgiven much.[19] Again the words of Jesus serve as a reminder that God's ways are not our ways and His thoughts are not our thoughts.[20]

A Woman's Wisdom

'Tis mightiest in the mightiest; it becomes
The throned monarch better than his crown;
His sceptre shows the force of temporal power,
The attribute to awe and majesty,
Wherein doth sit the dread and fear of kings;
But mercy is above this sceptred sway;
It is enthroned in the hearts of kings,
It is an attribute to God Himself;
And earthly power doth then show likest God's
When mercy seasons justice.

—Portia pleading the cause of Antonio,
from the pen of William Shakespeare

Mercy and Justice

Mercy is never at odds with justice. The preceding beatitude, which admonished believers to hunger and thirst after righteousness, has at its heart the seeking of a holy life. Thus, the call for exercising mercy would certainly not contradict that but would extend the challenge. The Bible itself admonishes its readers to combine truth and mercy.[21] Truth without mercy is pure legalism; mercy without truth is, at best, naivete. Without truth, holiness is not possible; without mercy, hope is gone. However, to link truth with mercy is to offer a plan for living the Christian life with the hope needed to encourage you along the way.

The Lord Himself offers the model for this unique combination. God is never less than just; yet His justice is always bathed with mercy. This mercy does not suggest weakness or indifference. In fact, mercy without justice would be to cover sin and wrongdoing and perhaps even degenerate to moral anarchy. Nevertheless, mercy does enable any sinner to make her way to God; it also offers comfort in the midst of the consequences of wrongdoing. By no means will mercy remove the consequences that come from sin; it offers immediate and complete forgiveness from sin. Mercy is never meant to minimize human sin or to vindicate the sinner; rather, it is to magnify God's love and redeem the sinner. A clear understanding of the magnitude of sin reveals a genuine realization of the unique love of God.

Every godly parent learns mercy early on. A child will transgress again and again. Sometimes these transgressions are very costly. Carelessness and rough play in formal areas of a home may lead to the breaking of a precious and priceless object; accidents and mistakes can tally to a high cost; wrong choices and selfish actions can bring shame and embarrassment to an entire household. Yet a Christ-honoring parent signs on for the long haul.

My friend June Hunt often reminisces about an incident from her own childhood. Her mother returned from a trip to find that her beautiful antique dining room table had been hopelessly marred. Young June, only four or five years of age at the time, had carved her initials on a corner of the table in an effort to add to its decoration. Mrs. Hunt explained to June that her carving was inappropriate for such a piece of furniture. Seeing the crestfallen face of the young child, however, she added some words that remain indelibly imprinted in June's mind to this day, "People are always more important than things." Just as the father of the prodigal did in Luke 15, a parent must correct, forgive, and restore. She continually extends mercy, and she never stops loving her child!

Mercy involves three tenses. It is based on the past action of Christ, who offered Himself and laid down His life for all who would turn in faith to Him. It is magnified in the present with hope offered and faith demonstrated, which enable you to get through the challenges and difficulties of life because of your faith in *His* faithfulness. But mercy does not stop in the present; it also looks to the future with its everlasting pursuit of the person in need.

When you extend mercy to another person, as Jesus did again and again, you are lowering the ladder of love to one who could never ascend out of her abyss without it. As a junior in high school my husband accompanied his parents on an around-the-world preaching tour. They visited war-torn South Korea. It was during the cold month of November. Following the war the land had been stripped of its resources. Poverty and suffering were apparent on every hand.

One of their most heart-wrenching stops was a public facility that housed the old and sick and the young and abandoned. The institution was understaffed and without even the most basic necessities. It provided only a measure of shelter to the most vulnerable people—the orphans and the elderly—who were its inhabitants. An air of hopelessness filled the building. The babies no longer cried because they had learned that it was futile. Paige and his parents were overwhelmed by the situation. They made arrangements to rescue the five babies who seemed most critically ill, bundling them up in their own clothing to transport them via a lengthy jeep ride across rugged terrain to the hospital in Seoul.

Their "mercies" were rewarded when each of those babies was snatched from the jaws of death. All but one were eventually adopted by loving families in the United States. Just as the good Samaritan in Scripture, they crossed the road of life; they dressed the wounds of the helpless in their path; they took the children with them and made provision for their care from their own resources. You cannot dwell near the cross without love and mercy finding you! And once it has found you, it will possess you and radiate from you!

Every woman is fighting her own challenging battle. She needs to feel that someone understands her trials and feels her hurts. She needs to know that someone cares whether she continues her fight or fails in her attempt. For you to season justice with the extension of your own mercy is to prove again that the heavenly Father's gracious dealings with you have not been in vain. You are willing to carry the light of mercy's torch, chasing away darkness and despair that envelop the life of others in the same way the Lord faithfully does this for you.

To release acts of compassion instead of unloading words of censure, to extend sympathy instead of revealing criticism—this is the better way. You need never fear any contradiction or polarity between justice and mercy. They met at the cross when the mercy of the Son was linked with the justice of the Father to provide atonement for our sins. There, too, His truth was bathed in the divine mercies so that you who seek to follow Him can reach out to the standard of His righteousness and make it yours through His grace.

When visiting Westminster Abbey, you cannot help but be intrigued by the many tributes etched in stone in honor of people who have left a legacy for future generations. One of those tributes is to the missionary-explorer David Livingstone. He died in the heart of Africa far from his family and homeland. He had shown love and mercy through his years of devoted service on that great continent. The African tribesmen who had experienced his mercies lovingly embalmed his body, carefully wrapped it, and then faithfully carried it over rivers, swamps, and jungles all the way to the coast. There Livingstone's body was placed on a ship to be returned to his native land.

The plaque above Livingstone's grave in Westminster Abbey reads: "Brought by faithful hands over land and sea, here rests David Livingstone, missionary, traveler, philanthropist." The missionary who extended mercies in the beginning received those mercies in return at the end! Those to whom Livingstone had ministered over the years were faithful to him even after his death. When you extend kindness to others, they are likely to reciprocate. If you do not show yourself friendly, you will likely not experience the kind mercies of others.[22]

Livingstone's life continues to inspire mercies. I remember just within the last decade that a student mission volunteer from Southeastern Seminary asked his beloved to meet him in London. There Donald took Lori to visit Livingstone's grave, the place carefully chosen by him for his proposal of marriage. There the couple pledged their love and commitment to each other and made their covenant to marry and then to serve the Lord beyond their homeland. They have kept that commitment and have planted their own lives beyond their native land in service to Christ.

Ethel Waters always blessed my heart with her songs and testimony. She seemed to exude mercy and kindness with every note she sang. Her personal testimony was heartrending, for her conception came as the result of the raping of a young girl, who became her mother. By all rights, and especially in the climate of the present age, Ethel would have been aborted as the reminder of a tragic event and an interruption to the life and dreams of a young girl. But by the mercies of God extended through her young mother, Ethel Waters was given life and love. She eventually found God's forgiveness and accepted Christ as her Savior. With her voice and energies she served the Lord, extending His mercies until her dying day.

Beware of making allowances only for yourself and your failures, but be quick to make allowance for others. Let your critical judgment center upon your own character and deeds. Use the mirror of the mercies of the perfect life of Christ Himself to look at others.

One of the kingdom ministries in which my husband and I served in years past was partially supported by the gracious gifts of generous benefactors. I had the privilege of maintaining a close relationship with a gracious couple who left their entire estate to be used in the Lord's work. The godly man had a lengthy and painful final illness. He was determined to leave all his affairs in order. He wanted to care for his wife and protect their vast estate from those who would try to take advantage of her in order to siphon off monies from their sizeable estate.

Though the couple had no children or heirs, they went to great lengths to make fair and generous distribution to distant family members as well as to friends and acquaintances. As I begged the dying man not to be unduly concerned with estate matters during his time of suffering, he continued to warn me that unscrupulous people would find ways to profit from the estate.

The day came when the gentleman went to be with the Lord. Our institution did everything we could to minister to his widow, including providing a student to stay with her. She became part of our personal family gatherings. The maintenance of her large home and lovely yard and gardens were all high priorities.

However, her husband proved to be a prophet. While my husband and I were out of the country, an attorney in her church persuaded the vulnerable widow to file suit against the Christian institution that had benefited from her husband's gift and against us personally (an act that violated the biblical mandate not to sue a Christian brother). The attorney inspired this action under the pretense that the woman should retrieve and manage the vast estate herself. Since she was not physically or mentally able to manage her household without assistance, the attorney offered to manage her financial affairs—for a fee!

There were tax complications, huge legal bills for our institution as well as for her personally. Most of all, the widow herself suffered because those who had faithfully cared for her were restrained from continuing many of their services to her because of legal liabilities.

In the end, an out-of-court settlement was made with the attorney; the widow was again our responsibility; the estate had been drained of a sizable amount; and the innocent widow carried an enormous amount of guilt until her death. Every time we were together she would cry pitifully, begging me to forgive her. None of my assurances seemed to relieve her of this burden, but we continued to do what we could to extend mercy.

In reality it was mercy that began the whole cycle. An elderly couple had no children; they lived simply. My husband and I had no idea they were prosperous and wealthy, but we knew they were lonely. We responded to their loneliness. God used that to open their hearts; we continued to extend mercy; God poured out blessings through them upon our institution. Even after the hurt and tragedy of being sued when we attempted only to help, God gave us the grace to extend mercy to this widow until her own death more than a decade after her husband died.

A Word of Wisdom

"Happy are the ones who love others as much when they are sick and not able to help them as when they are well and able to carry part of the burden."

—Francis of Assisi

To be merciful is an impossible task in your own strength. Only when Christ lives in you, when you share His nature, when you have His mind in you, can you share His tender heart and model His willingness to forgive. This attitude of mercy comes as a gift through the power of the Holy Spirit, who prepares and lives within the heart of the believer.

Remember the natural progression found in this challenging lifestyle described in Matthew 5: You determine to be humble or poor in spirit; in meekness you realize your helplessness; you mourn over the sinfulness of your own heart; you hunger and thirst after the reconciliation that comes from seeking His righteousness; all of this in your own heart and life then changes your outlook and attitude toward others so that you feel a sense of sorrow for all who helplessly flounder about in the labyrinth of sin. Because your own pride has been crushed, you are not concerned about your rights but have the desire to reach out to others in love and forgiveness. You realize what God has done for you despite what you deserve. You are ready to extend mercy.

The apostle Paul had a similar experience with Onesiphorus, whom Paul remembered as a person who came to meet his needs while he was in prison. Onesiphorus had compassion for the great apostle and wanted to encourage Paul as well as meet the apostle's physical needs. He did so in a gracious and loving way.[23]

Love and Mercy: The Linking of Heart and Hand

Love covers a lot more territory than mercy. Genuine love is a presence in good times or bad. Love is a friend to its recipient; love responds to another out of affection that is ready to share everything. Mercy, on the other hand, is like the doctor who may be a stranger or at most a mere acquaintance. He makes a house call when you are sick. The drive to mercy may not be merely via tender affection, but rather it may be a conscience pricked by need. Mercy is an offer of help even for a moment; love is the giving of a heart for the long term. Both offer healing and meet needs; both are in a way intertwined, but each operates within its own sphere.

Both love and mercy come from a work of grace in the individual heart. It is this grace, as well as the love for the Savior it inspires, that will compel you to acts of mercy.[24] Nothing in our yard at Magnolia Hill is any more pleasing to my senses of sight and smell than our rose garden. However, these wonderful roses, though a gift from God in their beauty and fragrance, did not just appear. The seedlings were carefully planted; and before they bloomed, they took root deep within the heart of the soil. Once the roots were down, the roses seem compelled to come forth. Pests and drought and creeping weeds have been repelled in order for the roses to shed their "merciful" ministry to me and others who enjoy their lovely and scented blooms.

Anyone who is void of compassion and unable to administer mercy must be unaware of divine grace. To recognize your human sinfulness and experience His divine forgiveness should make any woman merciful. When you experience the working of divine grace in your own life, you will be unable to refrain from serving as a conduit of that mercy in the lives of others.

How can an ordinary woman extend mercy to others? She begins by stepping into the shoes of another woman, feeling her pain, sensing her uncertainties, seeing her world crumble. Then and only then can she begin to live her life and think her thoughts and fight her battles. You don't put yourself into the life of another in a brief moment but rather by living your life in her shadow and trying over a period of time to walk where she walks and feel what she feels.

On more than one occasion I have gone to the bedside or to the home of a seminary student wife who has lost a baby through the tragedy of miscarriage. When I enter the sanctuary of grief in which that sweet mother dwells, I suddenly find that I am not there officially as the wife of the seminary president; rather, I come to the side of that grief-stricken woman as one who can still remember the same loss in my own life. I have experienced that hurt; I've asked the Lord those same searching questions; I've felt that same void. I can put myself in her place; I can stand in her shoes; I can experience the entire gamut of emotions—everything from hurt to anger to disillusionment and finally to the peace that passeth all understanding! What this woman needs, just as did I more than three decades ago, is mercy—a loving touch from someone who knows what a huge loss she has experienced.[25]

A wonderful example of such an extension of mercy is found in Matthew 25. The Lord addresses the judgment of the nations and makes the point that whatever is done for another in His name is the same as doing it for Him.[26] Those people who performed acts of mercy did not see Jesus; they received no face-to-face directive from Him; yet they acted in His behalf. He promised that they would receive the same reward they would have received if they had done the acts directly for Him. Such acts of mercy did not require great planning; they were the natural result of living a life patterned after the Lord. In other words, whatever mercy they extended was inspired by and related to Him.

You receive Christ and His mercy; a natural result to this is to show the same mercy to others. This mercy extended, in turn, opens you to receive still more mercy from the Lord whom you honor. The latter mercy is above and beyond the mercy found in regeneration or salvation; it becomes a reward for your faithfulness. But the chain does not stop there. You will also find that in extending mercy to others, those to whom you extend mercies are also moved to gratitude as they do not forget your Christian mercies in their behalf.

My files hold some meaningful letters expressing such gratitude for small expressions of mercy the Lord has allowed me to extend— brief notes I've written to people who have experienced losses, simple baskets I've sent to someone hospitalized over a lengthy period, treats from home I've taken to a missionary family in another country, a meal I've delivered to a new mother, an intercessory prayer I've uttered in a time of crisis.[27] Giving generously and continuously in the name of the Lord brings showers of blessings as well as manifold mercies.[28]

A Double Blessing

This beatitude carries a double blessing because both the giver and the receiver reap a reward. In the beginning the call to be merciful is a reference to Christian duty, but at the end it stands as a reward.[29] The Shunammite woman extended her mercy to the prophet Elijah. Then the Lord poured out His mercy through the prophet's kindness to her in another way.[30] She extended the hospitality of her home to the prophet; he was used by the Lord to restore the life of her dead son.

Mercy links liberality with utility. It is not only the doing of what needs to be done but doing the deed with the effusion prompted by a godly heart. God's mercy is so sweet that He always notes and rewards the kindness and mercy we extend to others.[31] You never lose with God.[32] The reward is not only in this life but also in the life to come.

A Prayer

I prayed: "O Lord, bless all the world,
And help me do my part."
And straightway He commanded me
To bind a broken heart.
I prayed, "Oh, bless each hungry child,
May they be amply fed."
He said, "Go find a starving soul,
And share with him your bread."
"Oh, stir the hearts of men," I prayed,
"And make them good and true."
He answered, "There is but one way—
They must be stirred through you."
Dear friend, unless you really mean
Exactly what you say,
Until you mean to work with God,
It's dangerous to pray.

—Leola Archer

Surely there is no character quality any more precious to the Lord than the willingness to exercise mercy.[33] Mercy is intricately woven into the Lord's being and is a trait of His holiness. Mercy is an accurate means for measuring godliness since its source is bound up in the nature of God Himself. It is the essence of His deity. His mercy never looks for payment or reward.[34] When you extend mercy, let it not be as something earned or deserved by another. Neither let it be as a reciprocal act based on something you received. Rather, let it be the overflowing of God's love within, a manifestation of an abiding attitude of mercy.[35] Such a spirit is contagious; it is more quickly caught than taught; it goes beyond the spiritual mind-set to the practical outworking.

Even when you cannot do much, do what you can. Some may have the resources to build churches or hospitals, to endow academic chairs or fund scholarships. I am not gainfully employed with a regular income; I do not have great personal wealth. Though I occasionally receive honorariums for speaking or royalty checks for my writings, my husband provides what I need as well as many things I want, and he gives me the opportunity to participate in our joint giving.

However, often my heart longs to give more. Through the years I have found great joy and deep satisfaction in giving my time and energies and creativity to the kingdom of Christ. The widow put her "two mites" into the temple treasury[36] and was commended not for the amount she gave but for the attitude of her heart that prompted her to give so sacrificially. In the same way, I can give myself to the Lord.[37] I can reach out and touch those who are hurting; I can pray for them; I can encourage others to respond to needs; I am responsible only to do what I can! By extending my mercies to others, I please Him.

Prayer and Meditation

O Lord, I remember the account of my sister Elizabeth who conceived a son in her old age. I am reminded by her testimony how graciously the Lord pours out His mercies upon women who love and honor Him. Just as the relatives and neighbors of Elizabeth noted this mercy in her life and rejoiced with her in the gift of a son in her old age,[38] I also praise you for the times in my life when your mercies have been poured out on me. I, too, was considered physically unable to conceive; yet You, O Lord, looked upon me with mercy and gave me a son and a daughter. Just like Elizabeth, with a grateful heart I have given them back to you. Lord, please continue to bestow on me, and my sisters who also cry out to You, abundant mercies. And, Lord, make me a vessel to extend Your mercies to those whom You bring into my life.

Moments for Enrichment

A VERSE TO MEMORIZE

"Let us therefore come boldly to the throne of grace, that we may obtain mercy and find grace to help in time of need" (Heb. 4:16).

ACTIVITIES TO ENHANCE YOUR UNDERSTANDING OF THE TEXT

1. Use a concordance to trace throughout Scripture the development of mercy both as a divine attribute and as a character quality of a person who seeks to have a distinctively Christian lifestyle.

2. Develop a chart of pertinent passages from both the Old and New Testaments to trace how this quality of mercy is to be used in the life of the believer.

3. Write your own definition of mercy based upon what you have learned in Scripture.

4. Determine the biblical prerequisites for extending mercy.

5. Chart a course for yourself, using biblical references, to develop a spirit of mercy and then extend mercies to others.

Mandate	Biblical Text	Action

Notes

1. Luke 1:6.
2. Exod. 15:20.
3. Num. 12:13.
4. Exod. 1:17.
5. Exod. 1:21.
6. Luke 18:13.
7. Rom. 5:8.
8. Matt. 25:31–46.
9. Prov. 21:21.
10. Prov. 11:17; 14:21.
11. See Mark 3:1–6.
12. See 1 John 4:7–8, 11–12, 20–21.
13. John 11:35.
14. Gal. 2:20.
15. Matt. 7:1–5.
16. Matt. 18:23–35.
17. John 8:1–11.
18. 1 Chron. 16:34.
19. Luke 7:44–47.
20. Isa. 55:8–9.
21. Ps. 25:10; 61:7; 85:10; Prov. 3:3.
22. Prov. 18:24.
23. 2 Tim. 1:16–18.
24. 2 Cor. 5:14.
25. 2 Cor. 1:3–4.
26. Matt. 25:35–36.
27. See Ps. 41:1–2.
28. Matt. 7:2.
29. See 2 Sam. 22:26; Ps. 37:26; 41:1.
30. 2 Kings 4:8–37.
31. Deut. 15:10; Ps. 37:26.
32. Heb. 6:10.
33. James 1:27.
34. See Matt. 10:42.
35. Prov. 11:25.
36. Luke 21:1–4.
37. Mic. 7:18.
38. Luke 1:58.

✣ 6 ✣

Leaving the Herd

BE HOLY:
LET YOUR ATTITUDE REFLECT A
SET-APART LIFESTYLE

The Context: Matthew 5:3–12

**"Blessed are the pure in heart,
For they shall see God."**

MATTHEW 5:8

The progression continues as the individual, who has recognized that her helplessness, her sinfulness, her battle with sin, and her resignation to the will of God, can never be self-satisfied because she has the constant desire to be filled with Christ. This filling comes through a supernatural growth process that builds character. It is only natural that such a state of blessedness would have a new purposefulness to demonstrate the qualities found in the life of the Lord Himself: mercy, purity of heart, and peace.

On an obscure island some of the most unique and expensive vases in the world are produced. Artisans fashion beautiful vessels from their native clay. When the piece seems to be perfectly molded into a finished product, the potter takes his hammer and crushes it into bits and pieces. Then those pieces are gathered and placed on the worktable where the master artist painstakingly puts the pieces together and reunites them with melted gold. The final product becomes even more valuable as a unique piece of art.

For the believer, this purity of heart that establishes a life of holiness and set-apartness cannot be attained except to begin with a broken heart. To meet the Savior is not to sink down to a padded sofa and a lifetime at ease in your earthly Zion. Rather, it is to hit the launching pad moving into the orbit of disciplined living and committed service. To meet the living Lord and receive a new heart is a wonderful experience, but the development and maturing of the Christian faith comes only with brokenness.

God's cure for sin cost Him the life of His only Son, and the curing of your sinful condition will cost you as well. Just as Jesus humbled Himself and became obedient to the cross,[1] you must humble yourself in obedience to Him. In your brokenness the beauty of the Lord Jesus shines through with a new dimension. It is the same process as that of the careful artisan I described. He broke a beautiful vessel and then took the broken pieces and restored the piece to greater beauty.

The "pure in heart" are noted for a lifestyle that is different and set apart, not only in the things they do but also in the thoughts and motivations that prompt their actions. To be pure in heart is to move from self-control to conscience-control to God-control. It is an elevating and uplifting process for the believer, enabling her to partake of the holiness of the living Lord.

Purity will empower you and make you strong; it challenges you to godliness. Only the pure in heart perceive that where they are standing is holy ground. They can see God in the midst of all the beauty He created in the world. This purity is not the legalism or ritualism to be worn and modeled as an outer garment for all to see; it is purity of the heart, an inner fountain that manifests itself by feeding all of life.

It is easy to become so obsessed with ceremonial cleansing and precise rituals that purity of heart and correctness of life fall by the wayside. On the other hand, the challenge is to determine to *act* in obedience to Him, doing His will whatever the personal cost. When you act in obedience to His Word, His grace will enable you to walk with Him and to be holy even as He is holy. God's grace gives you what you cannot attain on your own.

The "pure heart" can be expressed as a "good conscience." Martin Luther said, "My conscience is captive to the Word of God." The person who fulfills this demand for purity of heart harbors no evil intentions toward anyone and chooses instead to pursue the good. Purity by definition is undefiled and carefully refined. God is glorious in His personal holiness;[2] He is the source, the pattern, and the prototype for all holiness. This concept of holiness is a reference to the radical difference between the Creator God and His creation—you and me!

Purity, or the divine "otherness," comes from refinement, and the path to refinement is through the fire. Sometimes God sends affliction to soften the hearts of His children. Pain, suffering, sorrow, poverty—these become the furnace in which the heart is melted and made soft by the heat of the fire. C. S. Lewis predicted that God will "whisper" to you in your pleasures and "shout" to you in your pain. It is the concept of "severe mercy" in which you know that the worst has already happened. You are then freed from the shackles of the sadness you have *already* experienced to look forward to the joy that comes in the morning.[3]

When nations mint their coinage, they must send each coin through the fire to soften it so the appropriate image can be affixed. Often this image is the ruling sovereign of the land. The Lord, too, wants to place His image, as the ruling sovereign of heaven and earth, on His children. This is often done most effectively through the fire.[4] How gracious is the Lord as He exposes you to the heat, while being careful to protect you from its flames. As the dross is burned away, believers emerge as pure gold, stamped with His image and purified by His standard.

One of the most traumatic experiences in my own life occurred in a local church setting where my husband was serving as the pastor. On a Wednesday evening after church, my husband asked me to send the children home with a sitter because the personnel committee wanted to meet with both of us. Neither of us had any clue as to the agenda for such a meeting. However, shortly after we gathered in the pastor's office, the subject was on the table. It seems that I had been accused of interfering in the music department of the church, and my husband at the time was seeking a minister of music. The committee felt they were being kind to let us know of the accusation.

Never have I been any more stung with hurt and disbelief. The only connection I had ever had to the music department was when my husband and I accompanied the youth choir on mission tours or when I had hosted events of hospitality for the church choirs in our home. In all cases, my involvement had been at the request of the resident minister of music. I was not involved as a participant in the music program and was unaware of who was under consideration for the current opening.

As soon as the subject was on the table, my husband ordered that the doors to his office be locked and that the committee be prepared to remain until the matter was resolved. The committee members were quick to affirm that they did not believe the accusation, which had come in a letter from a minister of music who had served the church before our arrival. He, in turn, claimed to be quoting two ministers of music—one whose resignation my husband had been forced to seek and another who had been a long-time friend as well as a colaborer.

The matter was resolved that evening with calls to the three men involved. I was completely exonerated. The underlying motive seemed to be to get at my husband in an area where he would certainly be sensitive. But my life had been shattered in those brief moments. I resigned all my positions in the church and for a time became almost a recluse in our home. I was willing to help my husband in his ministry and to care for our children. I would attend church, but I wanted no assignments lest I be falsely accused again or my husband's ministry marred because of me. The most overwhelming grief came from feeling in my own heart that the people who had served as a conduit for these false accusations were those who should have known me best. I had lived among them; I had served them even in personal ways; I had felt comfortable and accepted among them. I now felt betrayed.

In the following months and years, however, I learned valuable lessons. I learned that the only friend who never disappoints or hurts us is Jesus, our Lord. I also learned that through the deepest hurts can come the greatest spiritual growth. It is in those experiences that you must rely completely on the Lord to provide the needed comfort, healing, and restoration.[5] My healing came slowly, but it did come! Another lesson that became apparent in later years is that the Lord allows you to go through experiences that prepare you for greater tests. Once you have experienced His faithfulness, you are quick to turn to Him in future times of crisis.[6]

A Woman's Wisdom

"We need no wings to go in search of Him, but have only to find a place where we can be alone—and look upon Him present with us."

—Teresa of Avila

The Power of the Pure in Heart

Because your heart is the shrine for your affections, the crucible for your thoughts, and the home for your energies and motivations, it is the most vital organ of the body. Even in the physical realm, the heart pumps the life-giving blood through veins and arteries to sustain the body.[7] Life and health, personality and productivity are determined by the condition of the heart.

But even more important is the spiritual arena in which the heart is also the key. The heart is the center of activity for the Spirit of God. You cannot ultimately purify your own heart. God alone provides salvation through the cleansing of your heart by the blood of Christ; you become clean because Christ removes the filth and impurity of sin. However, you must partner with Him in obedience to maintain the purity He demands for His dwelling place.

Jesus Christ is paradoxically both a part and the whole of this purifying experience. External actions will not suffice. You must never be so distracted with concern for *your* image that you lose *His* image. The heart (i.e., the spiritual nerve center) must become pure and clean in order to direct the corrective course that will point you to a godly lifestyle. You must develop a single-minded devotion to the Lord, loving Him with an unconditional and all-encompassing love. You must love Him for who He is and not for what He does for you.

You don't achieve holiness by doing certain things any more than you cease to be holy by not doing certain things. Rather, when you become His, beginning inside your heart, He will bring such a transformation that His holiness will be made manifest in all you do.

My husband knows that I love trains. When we were in Canada for a meeting, he scheduled a trip for us on the wonderful train that crosses Canada. We rode from Vancouver to Calgary, and it was a delightful experience with comfortable seats, excellent meals, devoted service from the personnel, and some of the most magnificent scenery I have ever seen. In the process we passed a sign identifying "The Continental Divide." This marker noted the strategic spot that divided the continent, with everything on one side going to the Atlantic and everything on the other side to the Pacific. There is a "divide" spiritually that is even more strategic. This is the division between salvation by grace on one hand and salvation by works on the other.

Chrysostom, identified as one of the church fathers and one of the key figures in early church history, has been identified as the greatest orator and pulpiteer in Christendom.[8] His sermons are models studied by preachers until this day. No one was more respected during the days he presided over Saint Sophia's Church in ancient Constantinople (modern-day Istanbul) and through the centuries.

However, this great spiritual leader was plagued by feelings of spiritual inadequacy. He tortured his body by refusing heat during the cold winter months, by sleeping on a cold floor, and by denying himself medical treatment. He refused food for lengthy periods of fasting. In all these acts of denial John Chrysostom felt that he was pursuing holiness, ignoring the clear mandate of Scripture that the heart is the seat of direction for the spiritual life.[9]

Outer appearance is not necessarily a mirror for what is within. Southeastern Seminary has a unique gentleman on its board of visitors. Richard Headrick wears his hair in a ponytail, and it's a long one. His ears are pierced (note the amusing quote on the next page to see the possible advantages this may bring), and he wears an earring. He is most at home in T-shirts and jeans, which probably are the more appropriate attire since he often rides his motorcycle across country.

On the other hand, Richard has a heart for God and a purpose for kingdom service that are far beyond the ordinary. In fact, he and his wife Gina have taken on an international ministry to visit families who are serving the Lord in remote and dangerous areas, and they are doing it at their own expense. Richard Headrick has a pure heart absolutely committed to honoring the Lord. Though his outer appearance is a bit out of the mainstream evangelical stereotype, his pure heart becomes apparent to any who spend time with him.

A Woman's Wisdom

"Men who have pierced ears are better prepared for marriage. They have experienced pain and bought jewelry."

—Rita Rudner

The word *purity* (Greek *katharos*), which occurs more than twenty times in the New Testament and is also widely used in classical Greek, is used to denote everything from physical cleanliness to the absence of defiling elements. When my husband and I travel in Third World countries, we always take with us small bottles of sanitizing liquid. We use these profusely to achieve cleanliness of everything from our hands to eating utensils. We also purchase bottled water for consumption whether in the hotel or out in the market.

During our visits to Russia several decades ago, I remember the greatest difficulty was not finding protection from the totalitarian government but success in finding "pure" water. Tap water could not be trusted, and only locally produced mineral water was available. This local mineral water tasted like seawater. During those days I longed for nothing more than a glass of pure water. Purity is important to maintain your health, to avoid sickness and disease, and even to satisfy your taste buds.

This same concept has come into the English language via *catharsis*, a word transliterated from Greek and having the sense of purifying. The "catheter" is a means of cleansing the entire body. There is no purity in any area of life without cleansing. In the Greek culture, the word also often had the sense of freeing oneself from debt, describing one who was able to pay all his debts so that no one could lay a claim to his account. When Jesus Christ enters your life, He becomes the *katharos* by which you can discharge your debt.[10] This Beatitude expresses the idea that those whose debt has been paid by Christ on the cross will indeed see God!

Anna, the daughter of Phanuel, appears in the New Testament as an aging widow who apparently had devoted herself to continual service in the temple. Though she is called a "prophetess," no reason is given for this designation. Her deceased husband could have been a prophet, or she herself may simply have been a woman through whom God spoke.

When Jesus' parents brought Him to the temple for dedication to the Lord, Anna was there. She watched as Simeon uttered a blessing upon the child and then prayed to the Father that he was ready to die.[11] However, when Anna saw the child, her response was to bear witness of the redemption to come.[12] Anna serves as an example of a woman who lived "righteously, and godly in the present age, looking for the blessed hope and glorious appearing of our great God and Savior Jesus Christ."[13] Her purity of heart immediately bore fruit in sharing the good news of the gospel.

The Pharisees pointed to the criterion for genuine purity of heart by their distortion of this wonderful goal. They looked to externals—ritual and ceremony and deeds done for public view—to affirm their holiness, ignoring the clear biblical mandate that God is interested in the internals.[14] Before you are too hard on the Pharisees, take note that the Christian world of this generation is much more interested in a performance Christianity—busyness for God—than a holy lifestyle.[15]

The Pharisees were determined to measure purity and holiness by external, ceremonial criteria. They thought of this purity as ceremonial cleanness. They thought they were equipped to come into the presence of God if they fulfilled certain requirements. Even today there are blessings associated with water and cleansing. During a trip to Greece in early January, I happened to be in Athens on Epiphany, a holiday on which the Greek Orthodox churches celebrate the baptism of Jesus by John the Baptist. Their traditional Epiphany celebration includes the "blessing of the water" ceremony during which a local priest tosses a cross into the sea. Youths then dive into the waters. Whoever retrieves the cross is to receive a special blessing because of his daring act of devotion.

However, the psalmist David recognized that no deed equips a person to stand before the Lord. Rather, anyone coming to the Lord must have clean hands and a pure heart.[16] A pure heart comes from meditation on and obedience to the Word of God and not from the cleansing of outward rituals. Those who emulate this quality have surrendered their hearts completely to the Lord Jesus, inviting Him to reign in their hearts. They are totally absorbed and overwhelmed by their devotion to the Lord.

A Word of Wisdom

"O God! Thou hast made us for Thyself and our souls are restless, searching, 'til they find their rest in Thee."

—St. Augustine of Africa

In the Old Testament, God is often described as being full of mercy. He calls for His children to adopt this same attitude of mercy. However, in the New Testament the religious leaders were often among the most scornful of those whom they considered outcasts.

For example, Jesus told a parable about the man attacked by thieves as he traveled from Jerusalem to Jericho. The priest and the Levite were religious leaders. They passed by the man without offering any help. They did not add to his wounds, nor did they try to take advantage of his condition by stealing his clothing or adding to his misery. They simply went by without helping him. They did nothing! Perhaps they didn't want to soil their clothing or defile their garments, which would have prohibited their religious service until proper cleansing had taken place.

Finally, along came a Samaritan. He was not considered religious by Jewish standards, and he was classified by some as an enemy of the Jews; yet he was full of compassion and extended mercy to the injured man. The unnamed Samaritan traveler became the hero of the story— not because he was religious or because he came from the same ethnic heritage as the injured man. Rather, he stopped and helped the injured man because the purity in his heart gave him sensitivity to one who was in need.[17]

One of my son's favorite movies has always been *Ben Hur,* the epic based on the novel written by General Lew Wallace, whose reading of the Bible moved him from an agnostic who doubted the existence of God to a believer who professed faith in Christ. As a result of his dramatic conversion, Wallace wrote the classic saga in which the hero Judah Ben Hur was arrested and sentenced to ship galleys for life because of his rebellion against Rome. As Ben Hur was dragged through the village of Nazareth on the way to the coast, he met Jesus at a well. Obviously Jesus was set apart by His response to Ben Hur. Often what seems coincidence to the human mind is God's way of staying anonymous.

General Wallace follows the text of Scripture so closely that he honors the long years of silence between Jesus' days in the temple at the age of twelve and His public ministry, which began at age thirty. General Wallace shows the merciful heart of Christ without putting a word into the mouth of the Savior. Jesus offered a drink of water to Ben Hur as he lay in the dust exhausted and discouraged. The mercy Jesus extended is all the more apparent because it is in contrast to the cruel inhumanity of the Romans. Jesus showed that these qualities are illustrated better in an individual's lifestyle than in her spoken words!

A Woman's Wisdom

"All the spiritual writers of past generations have recognised [sic] this joy in God, and all of them have written concerning the stripping process that seems necessary to bring us to it. They have called this process by different names, some calling it 'inward desolation,' and some the 'winter of the soul,' . . . but all meaning one and the same thing; and that thing is the experience of finding all earthly joys stained or taken away, in order to drive the soul to God alone."

—Hannah Whitall Smith

Indeed, every woman experiences this "winter of the soul." For most of you it comes around frequently enough to be seasonal! When those times come, they serve as a means of drawing you to the Lord Jesus just as the warmth of a roaring fire would pull you from the grip of a chilly room and surround your body as a warm cloak, bringing the security of comfort and the promise of renewed strength.

Still in my memory are several "winter" seasons in my own life. In each case, the Lord used our children to pull me to Him. I remember when our daughter married in 1992, we were coming to the end of a very painful experience in our lives and ministry. It had affected our entire family and extended over several years. With a hurting heart from the pain of that experience and the difficulty in knowing that our daughter would never live at home again, we were facing a challenging transition geographically as well as in the new ministry before us.

Shortly after we arrived in North Carolina to begin our new assignment, our daughter and son-in-love returned from their honeymoon. Graciously the Lord had directed them to Southeastern Seminary for Mark to complete his degrees. But in addition to the bonus of getting to see them with some regularity, I received from my precious daughter a wonderful album of memories, which I often refer to as one of my "ebenezers" (Hebrew *eben ezer*, literally "stone of help").[18] There were photographs of all the events leading up to and including the wedding as well as sweet notes of gratitude and encouragement for me. I still keep that album close by so that when I have a surge of homesickness for my Carmen, I can pick it up and feel close to her!

On another occasion after our move to the seminary, I got up wearily on a December morning. It happened to be the winter graduation day. I was in the final days of editing the *Woman's Study Bible*, and I was working long hours. When the family went out to eat or enjoyed some other special fellowship experience, I remained at my desk with only the company of my granddog A. J. In addition, suddenly a number of spider bites had appeared on my arm and hand—evidently a night assault—leaving me with aches and swelling!

As I sat down for my bowl of cereal before dressing for the commencement service, I had only a few bites before one of my teeth fell out—a new experience for me! I then entered my pity party with bitter crying and hopelessness.

My husband had already gone to the campus; so I went to my desk to look for a telephone number for the dentist. There on my desk was a delightful presentation, lovingly arranged by our son Armour after I had retired the preceding night. It included a Noah's Ark teapot and some other unique tea accessories.

For years I had carried on a tradition of hiding special gifts for our children on each of the twelve days leading up to Christmas. I had used the mystery of this experience to heighten their anticipation and add to the excitement of our favorite holiday. Sometimes it was a treasure hunt with tape-recorded clues; the gifts could also be delivered to them at school (like pizza for them and their friends during lunch break); the gifts could simply appear at the child's table, desk, or some other spot. They seemed to love this tradition even as young adults.

Now my son had turned the tables and prepared some surprises on these pre-Christmas days for me; this gloomy day was the first day of a trail of gifts.

What timing! Again God sent a ministering angel in my "winter season." One of the best antidotes for this "winter season in your soul" is to link yourself with the living Lord continually and consistently. I find personal solace in my "winter seasons" in the quiet times I set aside to wait before the Lord and to allow Him to cleanse and purify my heart so that He can fill it with His comforting Spirit. In those times, I walk while I talk to the Lord; then He talks to me while I walk through Scripture!

If you were to survey all the hospitals and institutions offering mercy and relief throughout the world, you would find that the vast majority of them were begun by Christian organizations. My husband and I were recently with an Oklahoma pastor. His congregation had been hit by a series of disasters—the notorious bombing of a prominent public building, tornadoes, and destructive fires (including his own home). He spoke with amazement at the outpouring of love from the Christian community. We learned from him that even the Red Cross mobilization for disasters is heavily dependent upon churches to supply volunteers as well as food, clothing, and medical supplies. Any genuine believer will be a conduit of mercy not only in her actions but also in the purity of her thoughts and words.

The emphasis of the Sermon on the Mount is righteousness from a changed heart instead of from obeying rules. This Beatitude seems to be directed, at least in part, to an individual's relationships with others. Perhaps it is best expressed in a practical vein as sincerity. In all of life, public and private, a woman who is pure in heart is transparent before God and others. There is nothing false in her thoughts. Even her thoughts and motives are unaffected by any base or devious thoughts.

I remember my friend Carol Ann Draper describing her mother-in-love as always having something good to say about others and conversely never having anything unkind to say about another. Carol Ann laughingly said, "One time she even had something good to say about the devil: 'He's certainly a hard worker!'"

Despite this admonition urging purity and transparency, many women are tempted to put on an appropriate mask for each occasion. The Greeks were noted for their magnificent theaters. Their grandeur consists of more than size, although there are some large ones like the twenty-five-thousand-seat amphitheater in ancient Ephesus. The theaters also have perfect acoustics, without the benefit of public address systems, and very efficient stages to accommodate their unique cast of actors.

In the Greek theater, one person played several roles. As he changed characters, he stepped behind a strategically placed column and changed masks. This playacting is the essence of hypocrisy, which is the English transliteration of the Greek word *hupokritēs,* which was used to describe an actor or one who impersonates another or assumes an identity other than his own and does so for audience approval. The compound Greek form combines the preposition *hupo* or "under" with *kritēs,* meaning "to judge" for the more literal sense of "judging under the mask."[19]

Once you begin to put on masks with deceit and duplicity, there is no end to the cover-up required. Women who are pure in heart will have a transparency with husbands, children, other family members, and all with whom they interact.

Only those who are pure in heart can see God because they are looking at Him through the lens of faith. The light He brings to darkness will reveal His dazzling glory in a unique way.

A Woman's Wisdom

"Where you tend a rose . . . a thistle cannot grow."

—Frances Hodgson Burnett

The Vision of the Pure

On the one hand, the Scripture states clearly that no person can "see God and live."[20] The contrast between the Lord's holiness and majesty and human unworthiness and frailty is too great for the two to intermingle. The glory surrounding the divine presence would overwhelm the insignificant countenance of a human being.[21]

On the other hand, the Bible records some awesome encounters between God and His creation. God began with His gracious determination to reveal Himself to His creation. He met Moses face to face;[22] and He made His presence known to the prophet Isaiah in a clear and unprecedented vision.[23] Perhaps it is understandable that the Lord would reward those committed to Him by accepting them into His presence.

If a man or a woman could see the infinite God, wouldn't the fact of His visibility rob the Creator of His unique infinity? After all, one of the mysteries of the Godhead is the incomprehensibility of the infinite nature of God. When the Russian astronauts reported that they could not see God with their human eyes, such information was not a discovery of these pioneers in space. The fact that after orbiting the earth they maintained that they had not seen God did not mean God was not there. Rather, it pointed to the fact that mere mortals are not able to see God (i.e., to confine Him to the dimension of human vision!) God describes Himself as a Spirit.[24]

The ancient Athenians recognized that God was beyond human comprehension when they dedicated one of their altars to the invisible and infinite unknown God.[25] God is not visible in shape or form to those whom He has created. Though you may envision Him through anthropomorphic characteristics, He is not as you are. He is not bound by time or space or by the imaginations of those whom He created.[26]

The "seeing" has both a present and a future fulfillment. In a sense God is so far from His creation that you cannot hope to see Him. Your iniquities have separated you from Him.[27] Yet what believers now know only partially and imperfectly will some day be perfected or completed.[28]

A Woman's Wisdom

"I need nothing but God, and to lose myself in the heart of Jesus."

—Margaret Mary Alacoque

Even in this life, the "pure in heart" are promised spiritual discernment by which they can see the divine character more clearly and understand the uniqueness of the Father's attributes. The God who is invisible becomes visible through the Son.[29] You see Him in all the circumstances of life and even in the experiences of pain and suffering. You see God when others cannot or will not see Him. However, the privilege of knowing God intimately and enjoying fellowship with Him is available only to believers through faith. Genuine repentance will always usher you back into the light of His presence and give you the privilege of "seeing" Him in all of His beauty.[30]

A Woman's Wisdom

"Begin and end the day with him who is the Alpha and Omega, and if you really experience what it is to love God, you will redeem all the time you can for his more immediate service."

—Susanna Wesley

Sainthood but Not Sinless Perfection

Some would pervert this wonderful challenge to suggest that the sanctification of a believing woman would remove her from the influence of the old carnal nature. But the Bible is clear that "if we say that we have no sin, we deceive ourselves, and the truth is not in us."[31] The history of saints in the Bible certainly confirms this: Eve disobeyed God and ate of the forbidden fruit;[32] Sarah encouraged her husband to take a concubine because her faith was too weak to believe God would keep His promise to give Abraham and her an heir;[33] Rebeccah deceived her husband and showed partiality to one of her sons;[34] Rachel lied to her father to protect the images she had stolen from the family;[35] Bathsheba committed adultery;[36] Martha let things become more important than people, even fellowship with the Lord;[37] Euodia and Syntyche, causing upheaval within the church.[38] In fact, the apostle Paul expressed his personal chagrin and continual struggle with the war within his own heart concerning whether to do good or evil.[39] Perhaps it is the evil that clings to the human heart that reveals the pure heart God wants His child to seek.

Nevertheless, holiness cannot be restricted to a heart that is without guile or deceit. The new birth imparts a holy or set-apart nature and links the believer with Christ through the living and sustaining presence of the Holy Spirit. This process of sanctification is put in motion and maintained through the indwelling Spirit. Justification is a definite, once-for-all, spontaneous action that never has to be repeated, but sanctification is a continuing, lifelong process in which believers seek to become more like the Lord (Acts 15:9, literally, *"purifying their hearts by faith"* or Titus 3:5, *"renewing of the Holy Spirit"*).

This process is expedited by denying yourself and your own desires on a daily basis,[40] by continually confessing your sins with sincerity,[41] and by determining to walk consciously in the way of righteousness.[42]

When you receive a new heart and a different nature through the process of regeneration, your heart and character are transformed through the work of divine grace in your heart. The resulting holiness leads you to undivided affections ("set your affections"), genuine sincerity of heart, and commitment to a godly lifestyle.

A Woman's Wisdom

"O my God! Imprint it on my soul with the strength of the Holy Spirit that, by his grace supported and defended, I may never more forget that thou art my all, and that I cannot be received in thy heavenly kingdom without a pure and faithful heart supremely devoted to thy holy will. Oh, keep me for the sake of Jesus Christ!"

—Elizabeth Seton

I once hired a young woman to be a part of my staff. We had advertised in local publications for applicants, and she responded to the ad. She immediately identified herself as a believer and expressed great joy in working in such a wonderful atmosphere. In the early months she expressed delight in coming to work and being a part of our campus ministries. However, one day I received a call from her pastor, who, prompted by a call from the parents of her husband, indicated concern that the young woman, her husband, and their young child were not attending church. Their names were on the church roll, but they were indifferent to participating in any of the church programs.

I took the opportunity to talk with the young woman about the importance of making the Lord an integral part of her home. I began to sense that she might not have established a personal relationship with the Lord despite the fact that her name was on the church roll.

Some months later, the woman abruptly resigned, saying, "You need someone who likes church to work for you." Yes, I do need "someone who likes church" to work alongside me at Magnolia Hill in the heart of the seminary campus. But before that person will enjoy being with God's people, she must have a personal encounter with the living Lord. When that happens, she will love to be a part of the fellowship of other believers. Women who bear the name of Christ must remember that in a sense they are writing a book through the way they live their daily lives.[43] Pure and genuine motives will eventually rise to the top; insincere and impure motives will be just as apparent.

The Beauty of Holiness

The gospel chorus expresses it well:

Let the beauty of Jesus be seen in me,
All His wonderful passion and purity;
O Thou Spirit divine, All my nature refine,
Till the beauty of Jesus be seen in me.[44]

A pure heart is one in which the fear of the Lord dwells. The beauty of His holiness is like a magnet pulling that person to the Lord.

The inevitable result is to worship Him and glorify His name.[45] Any woman with a pure heart will push far from herself evil thoughts and desires; she will be grieved over pride or indifference. She will constantly be casting impurities out of her heart and life. What remains will be beautiful and pleasing to all who look upon it.

During an impromptu television interview at a book signing in a secular book store in Romania, a news correspondent asked me an unusual question: "Why is your face shining?" The only explanation why such an impression could come from an aging and tired face like mine on that hot, humid day in the midst of a grueling schedule was "the Lord Jesus." He works from within, but His joy and peace and the purity of heart that only He can bring work their way to the outside as well.

Holiness (Hebrew *qodesh*) is the most basic attribute of God. It is that aspect of His being that unifies and summarizes all of His nature. It is synonymous with His deity. It makes Him utterly unlike any other.[46] Genuine joy comes from a taproot deep in the holiness of the One whose reservoirs contain an unlimited supply of the bubbling delight that brings true happiness and satisfaction. To immerse yourself in His holiness—in the beauty and sweetness of the divine nature—is to open the fountainhead of spiritual health and well-being and the joy this brings.

A Woman's Wisdom

Earth's crammed with heaven,
And every common bush afire with God;
But only he who sees, takes off his shoes,
The rest sit round it and pluck blackberries.

—Elizabeth Barrett Browning

Austria is one of my favorite countries to visit. Its national flower is the edelweiss, a German name meaning "noble and white." This perennial is part of the aster family. It grows primarily in the highest cliffs of the Alps, well camouflaged since its pure white blossoms blend in perfectly with the snowy peaks. Some people claim that the blossom will not even experience discoloring when it is picked, dried, or pressed for preservation. If this is true, you can see in the edelweiss a wonderful challenge to keep your own life pure, washed white by the blood of the Savior. Just like the edelweiss, you have the power to remain pure in Him.[47]

After a ruthless bruising from the hurricane and tornado that swept through our campus community a few years ago, trees were devastated. Just outside the chapel building an especially beautiful and majestic tree was damaged and eventually toppled, indicating that the inside of the trunk was hollow. Death and disease were already destroying the mighty tree even before the high winds of the hurricane and tornado. The lesson is clear: You need to check regularly the inside—your heart—and throw out the impurities before the trials and difficulties come. Strength within may counter turbulence without.

In Scripture, the wearing of a white robe is associated with coming into the presence of the Lord. There is not even the appearance of an unclean garment. The picture of purity is beautifully and appropriately portrayed through the bride's white garments. This purity represented in the white fabric is worked into a thing of beauty as the gown is fashioned into a flattering style.

Purification by Prevention

Scripture is filled with warnings that the pure-hearted followers of Christ will suffer attack from the forces of the Evil One.[48] Don't use your time and energies asking the Lord for a change in your circumstances; rather, ask Him to change your heart, which controls the way you respond to circumstances. Don't ask Him to manipulate the events of your life; instead ask Him to mold the character that would undergird all of life.

Those who are pure in heart are already uniquely prepared to resist Satan. They know his ways; yet they also know his weakness.[49] They also know how the final chapter will be written. They are confident that everything—whether bane or blessing—comes to them from the Lord, who will always be faithful at working the events and challenges of their lives for their ultimate good.[50]

Only those who are pure in heart can see God in the trials and difficulties of life. Only they can see affliction as a purifying agent of the Lord.[51] What is inexplicable in your time becomes more clearly understood in His time.[52] With this confidence, believers come boldly into the presence of the Lord, knowing that He is friend, encourager, and deliverer. They see God in the world He created, in the words inspired by His Spirit, in all the exigencies of life. A pure heart will lift up and honor a pure and holy God and actually see Him and His glory in a new and satisfying way.

My mother, Doris Weisiger Kelley, is a woman who is pure in heart. Family members who have been part of her inner circle, friends who have known her across the years, strangers whom she might encounter in her daily routines—all would agree that there is a unique sensitivity in her demeanor that sets her apart from others. Never a vulgar or profane word has come from her lips, never a questionable habit has gripped her life, never a word of gossip has been passed about in her conversations. She is known for her tender compassions administered to those who cross her path, and she is continually "losing her life" by emptying herself—her creativity and her energies—in self-sacrificing service to others.

As the woman of strength in Proverbs 31, she is praised by her husband and her children! You, like Doris Kelley, can't achieve this purity of heart in your own strength. God can do it for you; but you must want Him to do it! Holiness comes from God Himself; it is supernaturally breathed into a woman by God's Spirit. When you conform your mind to the mind of God, you can then enter into His holiness and see things as God sees them. Your soul becomes as wax to a seal, waiting for the divine imprimatur.

Prayer and Meditation

"Lord, I give up my own purposes and plans, all my own desires, hopes, and ambitions, and accept Thy will for my life. I give myself, my life, my all utterly to Thee, to be Thine forever. I hand over to Thy keeping all of my friendships; all the people whom I love are to take second place in my heart. Fill me and seal me with Thy Holy Spirit. Work out Thy whole will in my life, at any cost, now and forever. To me to live is Christ. Amen." (In 1925, these words were recorded by missionary Betty Stam in her personal journal. On December 8, 1934, Betty and John Stam were martyred by the communist regime in China.)

Moments for Enrichment

A VERSE TO MEMORIZE

"He who has clean hands and a pure heart,
Who has not lifted up his soul to an idol,
Nor sworn deceitfully.
He shall receive blessing from the Lord,
And righteousness from the God of his salvation" (Ps. 24:4–5).

ACTIVITIES TO ENHANCE YOUR UNDERSTANDING OF THE TEXT

1. A concordance will help you locate other references to the "pure in heart" in Scripture. These references may be charted as a tool for your own spiritual growth.

2. Consider the difference between rituals or religious practice and genuine acts of devotion or spiritual communion.

3. What women in Scripture have you identified as "pure in heart" and why?

Name	Example	Text
Mary, mother of Jesus	Desire to please God	Luke 1:38

4. Describe any contemporary women you know who are "pure in heart."

Notes

1. Phil. 2:8.
2. Exod. 15:11.
3. Ps. 30:5.
4. Isa. 48:10–11.
5. Rom. 8:28.
6. Rom. 8:37–39.
7. Lev. 17:11.
8. A.D. 347–407.
9. See Prov. 23:7; 27:19; Jer. 17:9; Matt. 15:19.
10. Rom. 6:23.
11. Luke 2:29.
12. Luke 2:38.
13. Titus 2:12–13.
14. Ps. 51:6.
15. 1 Sam. 16:7.
16. Ps. 24:3–4; 51:6, 10.
17. See Luke 10:30–35.
18. See 1 Sam. 7:12.
19. Matt. 6:2, 5, 16.
20. John 1:18; 1 John 4:12.
21. Exod. 33:20; 19:21.
22. Deut. 34:10.
23. Isa. 6:1, 5.
24. John 4:24; Acts 17:24–28.
25. See Acts 17:23.
26. Exod. 20:4.
27. Isa. 59:2.
28. 1 Cor. 13:12.
29. 1 Pet. 1:8.
30. Ps. 16:8; 17:15; Isa. 1:16; 2 Cor. 7:1; 1 Pet. 3:15.
31. 1 John 1:8.
32. Gen. 3:6.
33. Gen. 16:2.
34. Gen. 27:13.
35. Gen. 31:35.
36. 2 Sam. 11:4.

37. Luke 10:41–42.
38. Phil. 4:2.
39. Rom. 7:21; Jer. 17:9.
40. Matt. 16:24.
41. 1 John 1:9.
42. Prov. 3:5–6.
43. 2 Cor. 3:2.
44. "Let the Beauty of Jesus" by B. B. McKinney, 1940.
45. Ps. 29:2.
46. Isa. 40:25.
47. 1 John 3:2.
48. James 4:7–8.
49. 1 John 4:4.
50. Rom. 8:28.
51. Heb. 12:11.
52. Rom. 8:18.

⚜ 7 ⚜

More Than the Absence of War

BE A PEACEMAKER:
LET YOUR ATTITUDE BE ABSORBED
WITH RECONCILIATION

The Context: Matthew 5:3–12

**"Blessed are the peacemakers,
For they shall be called sons of God."**

MATTHEW 5:9

Biblical peace is more than political, social, and economic stability. This peace extends to a sense of wholeness, and it includes all that goes into your well-being. Though in history the term *peacemaker* has been used to describe a conquering ruler, the word is not used in this sense in biblical literature.

James described peace as the "fruit of righteousness."[1] In fact, he wove peace throughout the process of attaining righteousness by indicating that this righteousness is "sown in peace" and that "those who make peace" do the sowing. This description moves beyond political and economic stability to suggest a total well-being, which includes the spiritual realm of life. Peacemakers are not merely seeking an end to conflict; they want to bring healing among those who are alienated from one another and ultimately to bring all people to reconciliation with God Himself.

Progression is apparent in this pursuit of blessedness. The seventh Beatitude moves from character to conduct. The first four Beatitudes describe character traits. Believers are not to be self-sufficient (but humble), not self-satisfied (but mourning over personal sin), not self-willed (but meek), not self-righteous (but hungering and thirsting after God Himself). After equipping yourself with these character qualities that identify you with Christ, you are ready to move toward claiming the promises given to one who will follow this worthy way.

You will be merciful in dealing with others because you have been the recipient of mercy;[2] you will behold God Himself because you have determined to live a holy and set-apart life;[3] and you will be called "sons of God" because having experienced His peace you are eager to bring that peace to others.[4]

A Woman's Wisdom

He is our peace who has broken down ev'ry wall,
He is our peace; He is our peace.
Cast all your cares on Him, for He cares for you,
He is our peace, He is our peace.

—Kandela Groves

In this Beatitude of promise you attain the greatest intimacy with the heavenly Father.[5] Obviously you cannot be a peacemaker if you are not at peace with God, and you can find peace with God only through Jesus Christ.[6] Once at peace with the Creator God, you are ready to go into the world as His channel for establishing this peace in the hearts of others.[7] You bring peace out of strife and harmony out of dissonance only when you begin with peace in your own heart. As the peace of God is established in the hearts of people, the world will move toward peace among the nations.

War and Peace

In a sense war and peace go together in your spiritual trek. The believer is at war with evil and against the Evil One. At the same time, you who are committed to the Lord Jesus are experiencing the peace of God. In other words, you are affirming the Lord's demand for holiness, while acknowledging the cost of maintaining that holiness in the midst of a sin-filled world. In peacemaking, you must engage in spiritual warfare against evil and confront sin with strength and righteous indignation. In fact, there would be no need to search for peace if there were not a war going on. Thus, you engage in the most intense battle against sin and evil so that you can achieve peace and be a channel for this peace throughout the world.

A Word of Wisdom

Sure I must fight if I would reign;
Increase my courage, Lord!
I'll bear the toil, endure the pain,
Supported by thy Word.[8]

—Isaac Watts

The need for peace implies conflict. Peace may even demand war. Such confrontation is easily understood in light of the fact that believers find themselves in an alien world. The devil was the first peace-breaker. He introduced enmity between God and His creation.[9] The lack of peace results when something is wrong.

This contrast between war and peace can actually be visualized within the Beatitudes as a whole. On the one hand, the first part of each couplet expresses evidences of spiritual warfare: (1) poverty of spirit or helplessness, (2) mourning or grief, (3) meekness or submission to what may come, (4) hunger and thirst or desperation, (5) the need for mercy, (6) the realization of the importance of the human heart, and (7) the widespread suffering and persecution existing in the world (and especially among the body of believers).

On the other hand, the second part of each couplet describes peace in different ways with ideas like these: (1) the kingdom of heaven within the believer's heart, (2) comfort, (3) inheriting the earth as well as its natural beauty and resources, (4) being filled with the righteousness of Christ, (5) experiencing the mercies of God, (6) seeing God in His glory, (7) being called the children of God, and (8) experiencing the reign of God within your own heart.

Note that the second part of the couplets in both the first Beatitude and the last Beatitude express the same idea—God's reign in the believer's heart. In meditating upon the war that exists between good and evil and considering the peace God wants to give, you get a clear picture of just how important this peace is for the believer.[10]

Interestingly, the Beatitudes are interwoven in still different ways. For example, poverty of spirit naturally comes with mourning, since your humility helps you to see yourself as you are and thus to mourn over your sinfulness. Meekness is an appropriate partner to hungering and thirsting after the righteousness of God, because in obedience you passionately seek to know His Word and do it through the strength of God-control in your life by placing yourself submissively under the authority of the Lord. Being merciful accompanies the holiness born of a pure and undivided heart, as seeing God's mercy impels you to extend that mercy to others.

Finally, peacemaking is coupled with persecution for righteousness' sake, since reconciliation inevitably comes in the midst of opposition, and conflict can mean great suffering. Nevertheless, the total picture gives to the profile of Christian character a wholeness or completeness, which is the sense of meaning for perfection in the Bible.[11]

In another way of relating the challenging Christian lifestyle described in the Beatitudes, poverty of spirit can be linked with being merciful. Humility should prepare you in a unique way to be merciful to others. Mourning for sin is a perfect complement to purity of heart, since recognizing your sinfulness must precede the quest for holiness of life. In the same way, meekness or gentle self-control is a natural preparation for being a peacemaker.

To be a peacemaker means that you must separate yourself from your own interests, concerns, whims, and comforts. You no longer look at a matter in terms of what is best for you. Instead, you are looking at how others are affected and with concern for how the kingdom of Christ will be impacted. You are even willing to suffer injustice or wrong in order that Christ might be magnified and His peace might reign. The bridge that stretches throughout all of these life challenges is a recognition that none are possible unless God does His work of grace. You must wait upon Him for that which only He can give.[12]

The Lord is specific in the derivative form used within this promised blessing. He does not allude to "peace lovers" or "peace-keepers," both of whom would certainly be worthy of commendation. Rather, He precisely identifies this group as "peacemakers."

Yet this Beatitude is no defense of what is now called "pacifism." On the other hand, the challenge is not limited to evangelism in the sense that your only responsibility is to bring reconciliation between an individual and God. Rather, peacemaking is a lifetime process of reconciliation in which you are continually making known in every aspect of life God's redemptive purposes with all those who cross your path.

A Word of Wisdom

"Nothing is so strong as gentleness;
Nothing so gentle as real strength."

—Francis de Sales

Peacemaking is the climactic experience of obedience. Peacemaking is not the art of compromise. As the merciful, the peace-makers work to express to others what they have already experienced themselves. Peacemakers work to bring about healing and harmony among those who have been alienated. Sometimes keeping peace means choosing to endure suffering so others may be spared injustice.

Every believer has the responsibility to be a peacemaker. This Beatitude is more concerned with conduct than character. No woman can be a peacemaker until that peace has first of all become a reality in her own life. The reality of inward peace is based upon God's right-eous work in you. You dare not base such confident assurance upon your own strength,[13] beauty,[14] or personal righteousness.[15] To do so would identify you as a fool.[16] In a sense, you must die to self daily. In fact, this attribute gives completeness or wholeness to Christian character.

Being at peace is choosing to live in harmony with the order created by the Creator. Augustine expressed it this way: "Peace is the tranquility of order." You must love your enemies not because they *deserve* your love but because they *need* your love. The more you die to yourself and your own desires, the more you commit yourself to the Lord. When you are caring continually and passionately for your own desires, you are not able to make peace with others. When you think first about reaching out to grasp what is best for you, you cannot give your best energies and finest creativity to meeting the needs of others.

Peacemaking begins with an outpouring of love and generosity toward others. Loving even your enemies is a gift you offer to the Lord. Any wrong is best righted by spiritual means. No spiritual discipline exercised in response to injustice goes unnoticed and unrewarded by the Savior.

In my own life I remember feeling overwhelmed by an attack on my life and character, which, from my perspective, was unjust. The accusations were not from pagan acquaintances but from fellow believers. It was not a frontal assault but more like guerilla warfare. I felt helpless in bringing a peaceful solution and responding in an appropriate way. Should I try to defend myself, or should I simply quietly endure whatever came?

At that time, a godly deacon stopped me at church one Sunday and gave me a small card with this verse: "For God is not unjust to forget your work and labor of love which you have shown toward His name, in that you have ministered to the saints, and do minister."[17] That was my answer! What a peace to be reminded that God is not only very observant of what is happening in the lives of His children but that He is also in control. Nothing catches Him by surprise.

Sometimes you can best achieve peace by simply waiting on the Lord to work.

A Woman's Wisdom

"One of the ways the soul is supplied with delight is by seeing Me [the Father] work in the events of those you love. Wait and see!"

—Amy Carmichael

Nothing provides a better platform for peacemaking than purity of heart. Sincerity and openness provide opportunity for reconciliation. Reconciliation is not an option, since Jesus makes it clear that His followers are actually called to pursue peace.[18]

Peace in the Old Testament

The Hebrews, even from the Old Testament period, have used *shalom* (Hebrew, literally "peace") as their common greeting. This greeting is used in Scripture.[19] If you travel to Israel, you will be welcomed throughout the tiny nation with this familiar greeting. "Peace" used in this way means more than "hello." It encompasses the idea of wishing for you health, prosperity, safety, and well-being.[20] This customary greeting extends throughout the Semitic peoples. For example, in Jordan or Egypt it is common to greet people with *salem*, the Arabic word for *peace*.

Peace can also express the end of war,[21] indicate a relationship existing among friends,[22] confirm the absence of conflict,[23] describe a covenant with God,[24] or suggest the security of divine protection.[25] However, its root seems to suggest completeness, wholeness, harmony, and fulfillment—ideas that carry the connotation of harmonious relationships with others and success in what you attempt to do. Quiet tranquility and contentment in the heart of a person or in the life of a nation are marked with a spirit of peace.[26]

The Old Testament also presents peace as the calm experienced by those who trust the Lord[27] and as an attitude to be sought by all who want to please the Lord.[28] Only God could bring peace to the life tainted by human failure and sin. *Shalom* then becomes the result of what God offers in His covenant relationship with His people—His presence among them.

Specific references are made to His "covenant of peace" with the priests whom He appointed to represent Him,[29] with the monarchs whom He anointed to rule His people,[30] and with His people themselves. Throughout history the Israelites went through cycles of falling away from the Lord and then returning to Him in repentance.[31] This covenant also had an eschatological dimension with His people in the kingdom to come.[32] In the Old Testament peacemakers like Abraham[33] and Moses[34] are also commended.

"Peace" is also at the heart of messianic promises.[35] The prophet Isaiah describes the messianic king who would usher in the time of peace as "wonderful counselor" or one with great wisdom and leadership; as "mighty god," an emphasis on His deity; as "everlasting father," which indicates the loving relationship the Lord intends to establish with His people; and finally, as "prince of peace," which expresses a culmination of the prosperous and harmonious life to be experienced by the Lord's people under His reign.

Peace in the New Testament

In the New Testament, *peace* (Greek *eirēne*) suggests a joining together, an agreement, a harmonious relationship, a carefully synchronized symphony. The word *peace* could be a way to wish someone well[36] or to bid a person farewell.[37] The word is included in the greeting found at the beginning or end of every epistle except James and 1 John.

Paul in his epistles used a greeting appropriate for believers. They would have already received "grace" (Greek *charis*, literally "unmerited favor") through Christ's sacrificial love, followed by "peace," indicating the divine presence within.[38] No one has peace without first receiving grace! Both "grace" (for the Greeks) and "peace" (for the Hebrews) are typical greetings. They are linked together in the New Testament in a greeting especially appropriate for the racially blended first-century church.

Historians have described the period of Roman history extending from 30 B.C. to A.D. 130 as *Pax*[39] *Romana* or "Roman Peace." During this time Rome experienced its imperial greatness and ruled the vast area stretching from Britain to the Euphrates River and from the North Sea to the Sahara Desert. The Romans did indeed establish peace within their borders, but the government maintained this peace through fear. It was a negative peace.

In our household we learned about negative peace through observing our dogs. Armour, Jr., our granddog, and Bandit, alias the "Squealer"—both Treeing Walker hounds and half-brothers—dominated our household for several years. My husband brought the younger dog on the scene after older brother "A. J." had been the alpha dog for some months. One night the Squealer went after something that belonged to A. J. We never figured out whether it was food or a toy that started the bloody conflict. However, fierce growling and turf protection followed.

To make a long story short, a tragic and bitter fight erupted. Had it not been for the protection of an electric collar on his neck, the Squealer would have been killed by the larger and more powerful dog. My husband finally separated the two dogs, and eventually their physical wounds healed. It also had become apparent to the Squealer that A. J. was indeed the "alpha" dog—the one who was in charge. From that time on, the Squealer respected A. J.'s position, but he didn't like it. And on occasion he would still challenge the older dog. We did not dare leave them alone together, and the happy play they had enjoyed in earlier days was suspended. Yes, they had peace; but it was born of fear and intimidation.

For years Rome dominated the world with unparalleled international trade and the technological superiority of an advanced civilization, with military prowess and world leadership, and most of all with prosperity and peace. However, by the third century, political anarchy and financial crisis brought the demise of mighty Rome. So the rise and fall of civilizations that prosper for a time but then disintegrate into conflict and destruction from within continue from generation to generation. Ultimate peace comes only through Jesus Christ. Inward peace precedes outward prosperity, and such peace belongs to the righteous who trust in the Lord.[40]

"Peace" permeated the unveiling of Christianity. Its message is the "gospel of peace."[41] Jesus' purpose for coming into the world was to bring peace with God.[42] The Father is the "God of peace,"[43] and Jesus is the "peace" of every believer,[44] and all believers experience the presence of the "God of peace."[45] "Peace" is their inheritance from Christ.[46] This peace is spiritual peace that resides in the heart but radiates to the world beyond.

The woman with an issue of blood approached Jesus timidly but with great faith. She not only experienced physical healing but also had her sins forgiven, receiving freedom from her anxieties and worries.[47] The nameless woman who appeared at the house of Simon the Pharisee is simply identified as a "sinner." Jesus looked beyond what the woman had done to her penitent heart. When she sought forgiveness, Jesus readily offered her a new life and the peace that would accompany life in Christ.[48]

Both of these unnamed women were healed as a result of their faith and then told to "go in peace."[49] Believers are to function as peacemakers, finding their example in Christ. They build quiet confidence in others through understanding and goodwill. They demonstrate love and inspire trust. They work at overcoming evil with good. They are beating their swords into plowshares.[50]

Peace is a valuable gift from the heavenly Father, and it becomes the vehicle for His blessing. Christ began a ministry of reconciliation,[51] and then He committed that same task to His followers.[52] Peace will not come of itself; it comes only from conscious, persistent effort.

Consider This Grammatical Note

The word peacemaker *(Greek* eirēnopoioi*) appears in the Greek text as a predicate adjective; that is it follows the verb and modifies the subject of the verb. In the New Testament this derivation of the word is used only in the seventh Beatitude, which gives it a unique emphasis. Here the word should be understood in an active and literal sense to identify one who does indeed make peace and seek reconciliation rather than being understood in the passive sense as describing one who simply endures conflict by merely holding the peace.*

Peacemakers are not just people who attempt to be at peace; they actually work at establishing peace, and their work brings results. The same Greek root, whether appearing as a noun or verb, is used frequently in the New Testament as well as in the LXX (an abbreviation for the Septuagint or Greek translation of the Old Testament). For example, the word describes what God has done in reconciling His creation through Christ.[53]

Satan is continually sowing discord, but the Lord works toward reconciliation. Because God is the author of peace, reconciliation is ultimately a divine work. Jesus went to the cross to make peace between God and humankind.[54] Jesus is the supreme peacemaker.[55] The essence of the gospel is also expressed in this word.[56] Peace is an invaluable part of the armor of God, enabling believers to walk boldly into their daily spiritual battles[57] as well as a mark or fruit of a Christian lifestyle.[58] Peace comes as a by-product of holy living and as a gift from God to protect the believer against the forces of evil. And to exercise peace is to find joy.[59]

Elizabeth Clephane[60] was a quiet, sensitive child, whose parents died when she was young. Perhaps that accounted for her great sensitivity to the needs and sorrows of people around her. She died at the age of thirty-nine, but through the brief years in her Scottish homeland she was at rest and peace because of what Christ had done on the cross and in her heart. Clephane described this contentment in the wonderful words of a hymn she wrote.

A Woman's Wisdom

Beneath the cross of Jesus
I fain would take my stand,
The shadow of a mighty Rock,
Within a weary land:
A home within the wilderness,
A rest upon the way,
From the burning of the noon-tide heat,
And the burden of the day.[61]

—Elizabeth Clephane

The sense of duty is part of peacemaking. It is not merely an attracti Christian virtue, but it is also an important admonition for all believers.[62] Peacemakers are ambassadors sent to establish and work out peace. Peacemaking is not merely a gift to be distributed among

the body. Rather, it is an assignment for every believer. Though the
world cannot deal effectively with its own chaos, the peace that Christ
gives will distill all the trouble within its borders in such a way that the
world cannot disturb it. Peace brings harmony to life. The world thinks
of peace as the absence of outward disturbance—a forced state of
acquiescence borne out of the fear of open hostility. On the other
hand, the peace of God comes even in the midst of the world's turmoil;
it is dependent upon your being reconciled to God.

When the relationship between God and His creation is restored
through faith in Christ, enmity is dissolved and peace is the result. In
some cases, the Lord may not choose to calm the storm in your life or
to remove the tribulations you face; He may decide instead to grant
peace that enables you to function within the storm and to provide
strength so that you can endure the tribulations. Peace with God
means free and abundant access to God. This access then becomes a
safe haven for believers in the trials of life just as a ship seeks a secure
harbor to ride out the stormy sea.[63]

Genuine peace will protect the hearts and minds of believers from
worry, fear, and anxiety. Such quiet confidence cannot be explained
because it transcends human reason, bypasses difficult people, and
overrides unfortunate circumstances.[64] The sharing of peace with others begins with the proclamation of the gospel. This peacemaking is an
all-out war against evil.

A Word of Wisdom

"Peace is the harmony of satisfied union."

—St. Gregory of Nyssa

Peace as Rest

Women throughout history have kept journals and diaries, using them to describe the rituals of life. Often these descriptions have included how they observe the Lord's Day with prayer, worship, and rest. Such disciplines restored them. Rest and solitude must always be included in the cycle of life for women as they seek to recrank their physical energies and replenish their spiritual resources. God Himself rested after His creative work;[65] Jesus went away to a mountain to pray;[66] Jesus offers you much needed rest as well.[67]

The Lord's Day now receives less and less honor in homes, churches, or communities. When our children were young, my husband and I established some "Sunday rules." The children were not allowed to play outside or to go on recreational outings on the Lord's Day. They could read or play quiet indoor games or sleep. With a father who had to preach two to four times on Sunday and a mother who was worn out from a week's work of managing a busy household, our children had parents who needed a restful, quiet afternoon once a week. In fact, our body clocks seemed to run down and need to be rewound every Sunday.

Why did I establish such rules? I wish I could say my own piety led to this different routine on the Lord's Day. Actually, I came to this mind-set as the result of my own childhood. I asked my mother what prompted her decision to confine five children indoors on sunny Sunday afternoons. Her answer surprised me: "I didn't want to have to bathe all of you before church on Sunday evening!"

On further reflection, I am convinced that the Lord prompted my mother and me to incorporate into our lives and into the lives of our children the importance of divinely appointed rest. The rest offers an opportunity to reflect on the Lord and what He has done for you. It also gives you time to recharge your own batteries—to be filled so that you can empty yourself again in kingdom ministries during the coming week.

To the Hebrews, rest meant cessation from all activity. When God rested from His work of creation, He must have remembered with delight all the work He had described as "good."[68] The Sabbath still offers rest from work, time to honor God, and an appointed season to reflect on God and the covenant He established with His people.[69]

Devout Jews, even today, dedicate three days in the week's cycle to anticipate the coming of the Sabbath, which for them begins Friday evening at sundown and continues to Saturday evening at sundown. The Sabbath then is the high point of the week. Observant Jews do not dismiss the Sabbath when the day officially ends. They use the following three days to reflect back on that special day. Then the cycle of anticipation begins again.[70]

In Jerusalem on the Sabbath widespread inactivity is dictated by the orthodox community but experienced by all people. Don't expect to order a milkshake for lunch or plan to drive a car through orthodox communities. Hotel kitchens will be patroled by rabbis to be sure no cooking takes place (foods will have been prepared in advance); necessary labor will be done by non-religious Jews or Gentiles.

Believers in every generation should honor Sunday as a day of joyful reflection on what God has done for all who bear His name. This means giving priority to rest and to quiet meditation on the things of the Lord as well as to participation in corporate worship.[71]

A Word of Wisdom

I was glad when they said to me,
Let us go into the house of the Lord.[72]

Peace vs. Appeasement

Some think of the peacemaker as a mild, inoffensive, weak, and even pitiful person. Others think of anyone participating in war as being against peace. How can someone wielding a weapon have a heart for peace? In God's economy the peacemaker possesses great strength and is not bereft of weapons, for a great spiritual war has plagued believers in every generation. God expects those totally committed to Him to wage an assault on His enemies and to pull down the strongholds of Satan. Spiritual right is stronger than physical might. Human force is often futile, but spiritual power is always awesome.

Nothing in the New Testament presents appeasement as a means for peace, nor is there any suggestion of peace at any price. Pacifism or passive restraint to avoid conflict is not the goal. Peacemakers do not take the path of compromise, since to seek peace at any price is to sacrifice principle for expediency. Proclaiming peace when there is no peace is the work of the false prophet and not the testimony of a believing witness.[73]

In fact, the peace God brings to His children was secured at a great cost—the life of His Son. The path of the peacemaker is the way of the cross. Ultimately, evil can be conquered by no other means. The only sure way to right wrong is reconciliation in Jesus Christ. Peace is always a costly enterprise.

Peace does not mean that you are immune from pain and suffering, nor does it suggest that you will never experience misfortune or attack, nor does it indicate that you are free to pursue your own plans. In fact, peace does not come because you are in the midst of favorable circumstances. Rather, you have peace in spite of unfavorable circumstances. God's peace comes because of the inner sufficiency that only He can give. This true peace is viewing life from God's perspective.[74] Such quiet strength brings "great reward," a satisfying and lasting security.[75]

A Word of Wisdom

When peace, like a river, attendeth my way,
When sorrows like sea billows roll;
Whatever my lot, Thou hast taught me to say,
It is well, it is well with my soul.

Though Satan should buffet, tho trials should come,
Let this blest assurance control,
That Christ has regarded my helpless estate,
And hath shed His own blood for my soul.

It is well with my soul,
It is well,
It is well with my soul.[76]

—Horatio G. Spafford

Those who are peacemakers must often open themselves to endure personal suffering instead of letting that suffering fall on others. For example, if you are involved in a misunderstanding or quarrel, you are faced with the option of a painful apology to the person you have injured or a stinging rebuke of the one who has hurt you. In fact, it is possible that your forgiveness is delayed until the guilty party repents since there cannot be full forgiveness until the mistake is admitted and confessed. True peace and genuine forgiveness are costly.

What woman hasn't been called to assume the role of peacemaker. She begins at home, extends her efforts to church, community, and the world, in the midst of all her interpersonal relationships as daughter, sister, wife, mother, neighbor, etc. Peace seems to be an elusive ingredient throughout the world. Believers know that ultimately there will be no peace until the Prince of Peace comes.[77] Yet you who know the Prince of Peace must faithfully work to be His emissaries wherever He has placed you!

Abigail is one of my favorite Bible women. She was married to a man described as a wealthy "scoundrel" or "fool."[78] Her marriage to Nabal may have been arranged by her family. One of this obnoxious man's biggest mistakes was to insult David, the future king of Israel. David immediately sought vengeance upon Nabal and his household. Abigail learned of the incident through a servant, and she immediately assumed her role as peacemaker.

This beautiful and wise wife respectfully and quietly dissuaded the impetuous David from attacking her husband and his household. She was not disrespectful of her foolish husband, but she did show tact and humble graciousness toward David. Her peacemaking saved lives and prevented David from shedding innocent blood. David said to Abigail, "Go up in peace to your house . . . I have . . . respected your person."[79] He recognized that this "peacemaker" changed the direction of his life.

A Woman's Wisdom

"Blessed is the influence of one true, loving human soul on another."

—Mary Ann Elicot

God's peace closes in as an armed guard around the human heart that is committed to Him. This thought reminds me of how much I love gardens. They offer a place of shelter and delight. There are frequent references to gardens in the Bible, beginning with the pristine paradise into which God placed the man and woman He created.[80] In fact, the garden became a metaphor for the first home. Gardens take time and effort, but they bring great dividends in beauty and pleasure and restful retreat—a haven for peace.

When my husband and I travel through the United Kingdom, we often choose to bypass the excitement of London. We do enjoy its museums, theater, lessons in history, shopping, and afternoon teas; but these attractions pale in comparison to the peaceful rest offered by the English countryside and especially the Cotswolds. Our favorite retreat is the Buckland Manor—set in the midst of beautiful and extensive gardens.

The village of Broadway with quaint shops and winsome tearooms is nearby; Stratford with Shakespearean plays is not far; Oxford and its libraries and universities are also close. But Paige and I seldom leave Buckland and its gardens! We walk its paths; we dine *al fresco;* we enjoy the breathtaking beauty and fragrance of its gardens. Best of all, we enjoy the peaceful quiet and restful solitude found within its borders. When we depart this lovely retreat, we are refreshed and ready to meet our responsibilities with new vision and vigor!

A Woman's Wisdom

"The relaxation, joy, and peace we feel in a garden comes, I believe, because man was created in a garden. Whenever we wander into a garden or work in the soil, we are, in a very real sense, returning home."

—Pat Schiltz

Unrest is held at bay because God's concern is for your innermost being rather than the outer circumstances in which you find yourself. Uniting churches in harmonious work and reconciling others to Christ through personal evangelism are among the challenges for a peacemaker. But again, this harmony in the church cannot be attained at the

expense of doctrine. Jesus not only prayed for unity among His followers, He also prayed for doctrinal purity and holy conduct.

God's call for holiness demands peace with God. Peace is not tol-
erating evil and consenting to sin. Rahab was a Canaanite harlot from
Jericho.[81] Her house was probably located on the wall of the city. Why
would the Hebrew spies choose to lodge in the house of a pagan prostitute? No reason is given. It may have been offered because of prox-
imity to an escape route from the city, or perhaps it provided a cover
for the clandestine activities of the spies. In any case, Rahab was
apparently the only person in the city to believe the spies.

For Rahab to make an agreement with the enemy was considered
treason, a crime punishable by death. But she looked for peace beyond
politics and nationalism. She recognized the difference between her gods
and the God of Israel.[82] She used the covenant name of Israel's God and
made her peace with Him. Then she was obedient to the Lord through
her loyal protection of His people. In pursuing security for herself and her
family, she became a peacemaker and obtained protection for her family
from the conquering army.[83] God honored her faith and granted her deliverance and peace as well as a place in the lineage of Messiah.[84]

Peace describes the prevalence of good over evil and the reign of
God in the hearts and lives of believers. Peace is actually one of the
most potent forces in the world. Sometimes a peacemaker must fight
for peace during a time of peace. Resisting evil should be done according to God's timing and always with the aim of reconciliation.

The Nature of Sonship

If you are not a child of God, you cannot be a peacemaker for God.
You must have genuine peace within your heart to become a peace-
maker. The nature of grace is to change the heart and fill it with peace.
You must love peace to promote peace. God calls you to peace.[85]

When you become a peacemaker, you receive the honorable title
of being "sons of God." But this is more than a mere identification or

label; rather, it is a public acknowledgment of your relationship to the Lord and of your place in the family of God.[86]

To be made a "son of God" comes with regeneration, but to be called a "son of God" suggests recognition by others that you are esteemed and valued as a "son" and thus identified as an heir to the riches of heaven.[87] In other words, it involves public testimony with all the rights and privileges thereof.[88] Such a designation sets you apart to the Lord.[89]

All children of God do not become peacemakers. To make peace is a high calling that demands spiritual discipline and maturity. Being a peacemaker indicates the kind of relationship you have with the Father. Your family likeness should be easily recognized. Whether directly or indirectly, you should have a likeness to Christ.[90] Inner peace brings to the believer not only the indwelling presence of the Spirit but the Father's approval and joyful commendation. Peace-making is a challenging calling that demands a high level of commit-ment. It speaks of a unique fellowship with the heavenly Father.

As a young child and even throughout my adolescence, I experi-enced the importance of family identification. As the oldest of five children, I felt a tremendous burden of influence with my siblings. My parents seemed to increase this burden with their frequent reminder of my position in the family. Often I would make a request and have it denied only to protest that everybody, or at least somebody else, was being granted the privilege requested. My dad's response was stan-dard: "Well, it doesn't matter what anyone or everyone else is doing. 'Kelley girls' don't do it!" The family standard had been set above that of the world, and it inevitably held firm under pressure.

The question has been asked as to why the text reads "sons" instead of "children" of God. In 1 John 5 and elsewhere believers are identified with the title "children." Though any answer is subjective at best, perhaps one possibility would be to understand the meaning of "children" as suggesting youth, and even immaturity. On the other hand, the designation of "son" suggests strength and authority and especially the idea of inheritance. Jesus, the preacher who delivered this sermon, called Himself the "Son of God"[91] so that the designation "sons of God" identifies peacemakers in a unique way with Him.

One of the best verifications of sonship is likeness to the Father. God the Father is called "the God of peace."[92] He sends out ambassadors to pursue reconciliation and peace.[93] Jesus, the Son, is the Prince of Peace,[94] and He is to be a mediator of peace.[95] Jesus entered the world with an angelic chorus proclaiming "peace on earth,"[96] and He left the world with "peace I leave with you."[97] The Holy Spirit is the divine Comforter who seals believers with His peace.[98]

Sonship expresses an intimate relationship. As a son, the peacemaker portrays the work of the Father in His task of reconciliation. The most important aspect of this peacemaking is the commitment to bring about God's redemptive work in the midst of a hurting world. The work of peace is sweet and blessed. Note biblical references, in addition to the Beatitudes, in which peace is linked to purity of heart.[99]

The promise is not that a peacemaker will be *made* a child of God, which would be a reference to being made in His image and likeness; rather, the promise is that the peacemakers will be *called* "sons of God." This suggests that they were already regarded as sons. In fact, the verb is in the passive voice to affirm that the sonship was already established through a divine act in the past. They are different from the rest of the world because they are the children of God.[100] In other words, to be called "sons of God" indicates having godlike or godly characteristics.

A Woman's Wisdom

"I do believe that God has answers for some and peace of mind for others when answers do not come, and that, one way or another, God . . . has the very best idea of how to bring sense to all the chaos of shattered dreams we see around us."

—Jill Briscoe

The struggle for peace in your life as a believer centers on the challenge of recognizing and dealing with sin. God's standard for believers does not allow for bitterness and strife. Lust and passions, your own appetites and desires, will disturb the peace in your own life. When you are crushed with a consciousness of your own guilt, only Christ offers the certainty of pardon and grace.[101] The Bible holds the answers to the deep issues of life. Money, position, success, drugs, even people—these lead to emptiness and frustration. A desire to have self-satisfaction and to have everyone else contribute to your own physical desires will destroy peace in your life.

A Woman's Wisdom

"If you want to keep peace and charity among you, let each one be willing to take blame."

—Venerable Thecla Merlo

You begin to move toward peace in your life when you examine yourself in the light of God's standards.[102] Then you must weigh what you see in your own life against what God demands. You dare not turn aside from the Word of God just because it reproves and corrects. In fact, that is exactly when you pull God's Word to yourself and shine the light on its truths.[103] If you admit your wrong but refuse to change, you will not find genuine inner peace.

A selfish woman is neither at peace nor is she acting as a peacemaker. To have an untroubled mind frees you to live in quietness, acceptance, and peace. Frances Havergal,[104] known as England's "consecration poet," reflected this peace in her own lifestyle. She lived only forty-three years, but she was known and admired for her dedication to God and service to Him and others.

A Woman's Wisdom

Hidden in the hollow of His blessed hand,
Never foe can follow, never traitor stand;
Not a surge of worry, not a shade of care,
Not a blast of hurry touch the spirit there.
Ev'ry joy or trial falleth from above,
Traced upon our dial by the Sun of Love;
We may trust Him fully all for us to do—
They who trust Him wholly find Him wholly true.

Stayed upon Jehovah, hearts are fully blest—
Finding, as He promised, perfect peace and rest.[105]

—Frances R. Havergal

Conclusion

Peacemaking begins with an attitude of love and gratitude. You first release your personal rights and then become other-person oriented. All situations and all people must be seen in light of the context of the gospel. A spirit of contentment is essential to being at peace.

You learn to control your tongue, which may mean that on occasion you cannot speak your mind or repeat what others have said when doing so might provoke conflict and inflict hurt.[106] You must never lower yourself to the level of the one who offends, but look to Christ for an example of patience and long-suffering. You must exhibit constant vigilance, self-discipline, and passionate prayer. You must look for ways to make peace.

Peace does not come because of favorable circumstances or the right environment but in spite of unfavorable circumstances or hostile surroundings. The inner sufficiency God brings is in spite of all else. And in the words of St. Gerard Majella, "Who except God can give you peace? Has the world ever been able to satisfy the heart?" Yes, indeed, the crowning experience in your obedience to God is the peace He brings to your heart.

Every time you call on Jesus, He gives an undiluted confidence adequate to cover you from head to toe. His words are clear: "My peace I give to you."[107] You must let go of depending upon anything else. Your attitude must be one of complete reliance upon God. His cloak encircling you is the unique peace only He possesses. That peace does not appear when you are struggling for your own solutions or pursuing your own plans. You must stop dead in your tracks and *wait* for Him. Find out why the peace is slow in coming.

Clean out the cobwebs of stubborn self-will and abandon any preoccupation of doing good things. Remember that problems between God and you are not the result of His inadequacy but the fruit of your disobedience. God wants you to take a seat in quietness and watch Him work to produce "the peace of God, which surpasses all understanding"[108]—a peace He created and one He alone distributes.

God's blessings are finished and awaiting an outpouring on all who abide by His covenant. He wants to transform your life so you will receive a quiet contentment that radiates joy and peace. When you reflect His peace, everyone knows you are right with God.

Prayer and Meditation

Come, O Creator, Spirit blest!
And in our souls take up Thy rest;
Come, with Thy grace and heavenly aid,
To fill the hearts which Thou has made.

—Mary Artemisia Lathbury

Moments for Enrichment

A VERSE TO MEMORIZE

"The wisdom that is from above is first pure, then peaceable, gentle, willing to yield, full of mercy and good fruits, without partiality, and without hypocrisy" (James 3:17).

ACTIVITIES TO ENHANCE YOUR UNDERSTANDING OF THE TEXT

1. Consider the pattern of war and peace in your own relationships. Set forth the qualities necessary for you to become a peacemaker in your own personal world.

2. Formulate your own theology of rest—physically, mentally, and spiritually.

3. How do you celebrate the Lord's Day in your home?

4. Study the following chart using the Hebrew custom of looking forward to the Sabbath, enjoying the day itself, and looking back to savor its impact on your life. Consider adapting such a discipline in your own celebrations of the Lord's Day. Note any ideas on the chart.

The Lord's Day

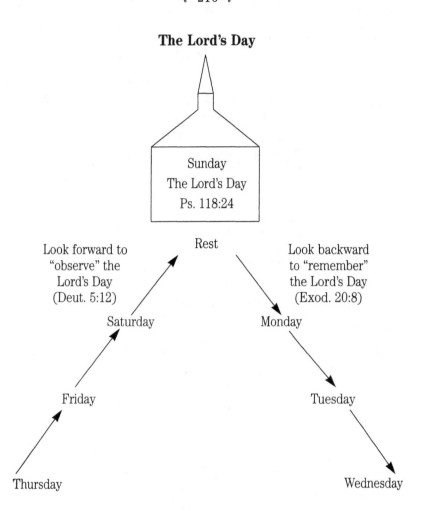

Sunday
The Lord's Day
Ps. 118:24

Rest

Look forward to
"observe" the
Lord's Day
(Deut. 5:12)

Look backward
to "remember"
the Lord's Day
(Exod. 20:8)

Saturday

Monday

Friday

Tuesday

Thursday

Wednesday

Ingredients for preparation for and celebration of the Lord's Day:

1. Regular Meditations on the Things of the Lord in Your Own Heart
   (Ps. 119:9–11, 33, 38, 97–98, 105).
2. Lifestyle Teaching of Spiritual Values to Your Children
   (Deut. 6:6–9; Ps. 78:4–8).
3. Productive Work Using Your Energies and Gifts (Neh. 4:6; 2 Thess.
   3:10).
4. Corporate Worship in the Community of Faith (Heb. 10:2).

Notes

1. James 3:18.
2. Matt. 5:7.
3. Matt. 5:8.
4. Matt. 5:9.
5. See also Matt. 5:45; Luke 6:35.
6. Rom. 5:1.
7. Rom. 12:18.
8. Isaac Watts, "Am I a Soldier of the Cross," 1724.
9. Gen. 3:9–19.
10. Spiros Zodhiates, *The Pursuit of Happiness* (AMG Publishers, 1966, 1998), 20–21.
11. Matt. 5:48; John 17:23; Col. 1:28.
12. Isa. 40:31.
13. Isa. 30:12.
14. Ezek. 16:15.
15. Ezek. 33:12.
16. Prov. 28:26.
17. Heb. 6:10.
18. 1 Cor. 7:15; 1 Pet. 3:11; Heb. 12:14; Rom. 12:18.
19. Gen. 29:6; see also comparable New Testament greeting, Luke 24:36.
20. See Eccl. 3:8; Isa. 45:7.
21. Josh. 9:15.
22. Gen. 26:29.
23. 1 Kings 4:25.
24. Num. 25:12.
25. Isa. 26:12.
26. Isa. 32:17.
27. Isa. 26:3.
28. Ps. 34:14.
29. Num. 25:12–13.
30. 1 Chron. 22:9–10.
31. Isa. 54:10.
32. Ezek. 34:25.
33. Gen. 13:8.
34. Exod. 2:13.
35. See Isa. 9:6–7.

36. Luke 10:5.
37. James 2:16.
38. 1 Thess. 1:1.
39. Latin *pax,* literally "agreement" or "pact."
40. Job 22:21.
41. Eph. 6:15.
42. Luke 1:76–79.
43. 1 Thess. 5:23.
44. Eph. 2:14–15.
45. 2 Cor. 13:11; Phil. 4:9.
46. John 16:33.
47. Matt. 9:20–22.
48. Luke 7:36–50.
49. Mark 5:34; Luke 7:50.
50. Isa. 2:4.
51. Matt. 5:24.
52. 2 Cor. 5:18.
53. Eph. 2:15.
54. Col. 1:20.
55. John 14:27.
56. Eph. 6:15.
57. Eph. 6:11–15.
58. Gal. 5:22–23.
59. Prov. 12:20.
60. She lived from 1830 to 1869.
61. Elizabeth Clephane, "Beneath the Cross of Jesus."
62. Rom. 12:18.
63. Rom. 5:1–5.
64. Phil. 4:7.
65. Gen. 2:2.
66. Matt. 14:23.
67. Matt. 11:28–30.
68. Gen. 1:31.
69. Lev. 23:3.
70. See chart on the Lord's Day on page 220.
71. Ps. 118:24.
72. Ps. 122:1.
73. Jer. 6:14.
74. John 14:27.
75. Heb. 10:35–36.

76. Horatio G. Spafford, "It Is Well with My Soul," 1873. This hymn was written by Spafford after his daughters died at sea in a tragic accident during a transoceanic voyage with their mother.
77. Dan. 9:24–25.
78. 1 Sam. 25:3, 17.
79. 1 Sam. 25:35.
80. Gen. 2:9.
81. Josh. 2:1.
82. Josh. 2:11.
83. Josh. 2:12–13.
84. Heb. 11:31; see also Matt. 1:5.
85. 1 Cor. 7:15.
86. Eph. 1:7–12.
87. Eph. 2:19.
88. Heb. 2:10–13.
89. Rom. 8:17.
90. Phil. 2:1–2.
91. Matt. 8:20.
92. Heb. 13:20.
93. 2 Cor. 5:20.
94. See the messianic prophecy in Isa. 9:6.
95. 1 Tim. 2:5.
96. Luke 2:14.
97. John 14:27.
98. 2 Cor. 1:22.
99. Heb. 12:14; James 3:17.
100. 1 John 3:2.
101. Ps. 139:23–24.
102. Ps. 119:165.
103. 2 Tim. 3:16–17.
104. She lived from 1836 to 1879.
105. Frances R. Havergal, "Perfect Peace," 1878.
106. James 1:19.
107. John 14:27.
108. Phil. 4:7.

The Tough Assignment

BE COMMITTED:
LET YOUR ATTITUDE BE ONE OF
COURAGE UNDER FIRE

---

*"Blessed are those who are persecuted for
  righteousness' sake,
For theirs is the kingdom of heaven.
Blessed are you when they revile and
  persecute you,
And say all kinds of evil against you falsely
  for My sake.
Rejoice and be exceedingly glad,
For great is your reward in heaven,
For so they persecuted the prophets who were
  before you."*

MATTHEW 5:10–12

The last Beatitude in the Sermon on the Mount comes full circle to the same reward as that promised in the first Beatitude. Jesus started with a clear statement, and He has returned to it for His climactic conclusion. The first Beatitude promises that those who are marked by poverty of spirit or humility possess the kingdom of heaven. The subsequent Beatitudes present six other characteristics of the believer who seeks to exemplify a godly lifestyle, together with the rewards for such set-apart living. The discussion is then brought to a grand climax with how this believer is to relate to the world in which she lives. The promised blessing is that she will possess the kingdom of heaven!

The Beatitudes might be best understood as human challenges with divine promises. Each one is a paradox. In other words, the challenge presented as well as the blessing promised is the direct opposite of what the world expects or guarantees. For example, mourning and rejoicing are both to be experienced by God's children. Hunger and thirst are running parallel with complete satisfaction for the believer. Contradictory feelings are being continually intermingled. What seems to be without solution for the human mind is easily understood by the spiritual mind under the guidance of the Holy Spirit.[1]

The Beatitude discussed in this chapter is more of a paradox than any of the preceding ones. Some interpreters even consider Matthew 5:10–12 an addendum or appendix to the Beatitudes as a whole because these verses describe what will happen to the believer, who seeks to conform herself to His image.[2] She is opposed by the world because of her determination to live righteously. Perhaps that is why the challenge in this Beatitude is presented in a more extended format with minute repetition, precise description, and clear application. In other words, with this double blessing comes a double challenge for conducting your life.

As impossible as the attaining of these qualities described in the Beatitudes seems to be, Jesus modeled them perfectly. He is humble;

He personifies spiritual sensitivity; He is meek; He is obedient to the Father; He is compassionate; He is the essence of holiness; He is the role model for making peace; He endured shame and suffering on the cross. No woman has ever given herself in service to others as much as the Lord has. However, some loved Him devotedly, while others hated Him passionately.

You, as a believing woman, can follow the Lord's example. You begin on your knees, laying your personal spiritual poverty and help-lessness before Him and expressing sorrow over your sinfulness and the sins of others. You then submit yourself in meekness to the Lord and His will, hungering and thirsting to know Him and His Word and to grow in exercising the fruit of this relationship. You move outside your-self to overflow to others, extending mercies, purifying your own heart, and becoming a peacemaker. God does not stop with satisfying your spiritual needs; He pours Himself into your life in such abundance that you can minister to others.

Once you have sought His ways and assumed His work, you will experience the same opposition He experienced, because your stan-dards will be opposed to the values of the world.[3] Persecution is not held in check until you have fully clothed yourself with these godly traits described in the Beatitudes. It begins the moment you make a commitment to identify yourself so thoroughly with the Lord that you seek to become like Him.[4] Then persecution follows, increasing in its intensity as you become more and more like the Savior. Service to the Lord will awaken the greatest opposition from Satan because the world is looking for ease and compromise, not gentleness of spirit and purity of heart.

A Logical Move

You may actually be persecuted *because* you are a peacemaker! In many ways it is quite logical to move from peacemaking to persecu-tion. Whatever you try to do in order to make peace is simply not enough for some people. Those who reject the Lord and His righteousness have no other choice but to clash with what is distasteful and convicting to them. Persecution is inevitable when there is a clash between two worldviews that cannot be reconciled. However, persecution in itself does not produce the initial blessing described here. Believers are persecuted because they have already been blessed, but their response to this persecution can result in further blessing.

A believing woman is not persecuted *because* she is obnoxious or difficult or lacking in wisdom and understanding or fanatical in expressing her beliefs. Yet she may be persecuted for any of these reasons. However, to bring suffering upon yourself for any reason does not entitle you to claim the promise of blessing in this Beatitude.

The woman who is persecuted because she is doing something unwise or wrong will not be blessed in the way described in this Beatitude. In fact, she will not be blessed just because she has suffered for a worthy cause. Persecution merely for being good or noble or even self-sacrificing is not what Jesus meant here. She will not be blessed because she is a certain type of person or because she possesses a particular personality. Rather, she will be blessed because she behaves in a certain manner and is committed to a set-apart lifestyle *for righteousness' sake.* Her determination is to maintain an attitude that reflects the essence of discipleship to Jesus. This righteous attitude, which means living like the Lord Jesus, is the reason for persecution.[5]

The Bible has many examples of just such righteous living. Hannah agonized before the Lord over her barrenness and her longing for a child. She endured cruel taunting from her rival Peninnah. Even Eli the priest falsely accused her.[6] Yet Hannah was faithful to live righteously and to trust the Lord even in her suffering. The Lord remembered Hannah and opened her barren womb, giving her a son who would also walk righteously before the Lord.[7]

An Israelite maidservant was captured and taken into slavery by the Syrians. Placed in the household of Naaman, she performed menial tasks for Naaman's wife. The young girl showed determination to serve her mistress well and even bravely shared her simple faith with her captors in an effort to help Naaman cure his leprous condition.[8]

Puah and Shiphrah were midwives assigned the task of helping the Hebrew women deliver their babies during the Egyptian captivity of the Israelites. These two midwives risked their lives by defying Pharaoh's order to kill all the Hebrew male infants. They were rewarded not only with their own security from the wrath of Pharaoh but also with God's provision of "households" for them personally because of their faithfulness to the God of Israel.[9] God does not disappoint women who trust Him.

My husband and I visited some of our students in a country closed to the gospel—a nation in which Christians are persecuted. One evening we invited the students and their families to dinner at a special restaurant. By what seemed to be an accident (though later proving to be a divine encounter), the friends traveling with us met a young woman who was employed by the restaurant. In conversation with them, this woman asked if they were Christians. She was delighted to meet and have fellowship with fellow believers and shared ways in which she had been witnessing to her coworkers. The next day she called to let us know that she had been fired because of her commitment to Christ.

Most people would have been despondent over the loss of income and the uncertainties prompted by public humiliation, but this woman had a quiet confidence in the Lord and His providence. By the time we connected with her that evening, God had supplied another job with an increase in salary; and all this happened on the day she was fired! Her confidence in the Lord, courage to stand firm for Him, and commitment to remain true to Him were present in her life long before she lost her job, and they remained apparent during the hours she was jobless. God walked with her through it all.[10]

A Woman's Wisdom

"Worry does not empty tomorrow of its sorrow, it empties today of its strength. It does not enable us to escape evil. It makes us unfit to face evil when it comes. It is the interest you pay on trouble before it comes."

—Corrie ten Boom

Suffering and injustice are not always met with a happy solution. Yet God is faithful to meet the needs of His children, whether it is to reverse their misfortune or give them the grace to bear their burdens. The believing woman's responsibility is not to find an escape from trials and difficulties. Rather she should make certain that her suffering is not because of her own wrong choices but because she is seeking to live righteously before the Lord.

When my husband and I completed college and began our seminary work, we moved from our home state and the comfort of adequate income and secure housing to the uncertainties of what seemed a foreign land. Culture shock came, since for the first time we would be living in a large metropolitan area. At that time, Abilene, Texas, didn't even have beer in the grocery stores, while New Orleans, Louisiana, had bars even in family restaurants!

No housing was available on campus. We moved from a parsonage adjoining the church to an apartment in a very secular neighborhood. At that time my husband had preached around the world but never in the United States beyond the state of Texas. No supply preaching was on the calendar, and there was no church employment on the horizon. However, we made the move, knowing that God was leading us to do so. My husband was also determined that I would attend seminary with him.

Paige expressed confidence that God would provide for our needs, and he was reluctant for me to undertake even a part-time job because of the allergies and asthma that plagued me. On the other hand, I reasoned that my business skills and teaching certification made it much easier for me to get employment quickly in order to take care of our needs until a church or some other opportunity opened for him. Within several days, I had accepted a position in the dean's office, arranged to substitute one day a week at a Christian school, and signed on to do inventory at a local department store one day a week. That left four days for a full load of seminary classes, including advanced Greek and beginning Hebrew, and Sunday to serve the Lord.

As you can imagine, I quickly broke my health. "Helping" my husband by providing some initial income was soon overshadowed by the expenses that accumulated as my medical needs increased. Even to this day, despite the gracious hand of the Lord, I bear in my body the scars of abusing my health during those years. I suffered many days, propped up in bed in a darkened room, gasping for breath. But this suffering was not *for righteousness' sake;* it was because of my own stubborn pride in feeling that I knew better than my husband what our family needed! Wrong choices can have far-reaching consequences.

An Invitation to Opposition

Because a believing woman is different, she will arouse opposition. Humanism, one of the philosophies making its way through the world, is determined to do away with individuality. A person who is unique may stand out, but it is to endure resentment and not to claim admiration. The world wants conformity to its customs and ideas.

Believers tend to be viewed as the conscience of the world. They are a rebuke to a sinful and self-centered lifestyle. Any genuine believer will serve as a living rebuke to what is sinful by who she is and by what she says and does.[11] Have you ever had a family member or friend whose presence pricked your heart because she reminded you of your own sinfulness? Just her presence could bring conviction over your wrong choices. She didn't scold or rebuke. She did not indulge in condescending judgment. But she always seemed to come straight from the presence of Jesus![12]

To become like the Lord Jesus is to become light just as He is light.[13] Light exposes and even, as it grows stronger, removes darkness. No wonder darkness hates the light! To offend the world, you do not have to be unwise in your choices or obnoxious in living your Christian faith. Just to be like Christ will bring persecution. The character of a Christian certainly gives a reading as to who she is, but her reaction to her circumstances of life also adds to her credibility.

Christians arouse opposition because they interfere with the affairs of the world and its pleasures. If Jesus were living in today's world, He would not be welcome in every home, nor would the doors of every church be open to Him. Certainly there are habits exercised and enter-tainment experienced that would bring a blush to your face if the Lord Himself were standing by. Remember how Jesus drove the money changers out of the temple because of their dishonest gain at the expense of the people?[14] Paul was attacked in Ephesus because he was ruining their sales of the images of Diana, goddess of the Ephesians.[15]

On occasion Christian groups have had difficulty securing hotel rooms and meeting halls because they were not expected to use the accompanying bars and casinos. Of course, being a believer does not necessarily mean you do not drink alcoholic beverages, nor is it a sure sign that you will not gamble; but these habits largely remain the exception rather than the rule among some groups of evangelical Christians. To fill a hotel with believers may interfere with business and cut profits!

Believers under Fire

Jesus made it clear that believers could expect opposition and suf-fering.[16] In fact, the author of Luke issued a warning to those who receive the praise of others.[17] The reception that believers receive in the world is expected to be hostile.[18]

My husband has never shied away from standing firm in his convictions, even when to do so meant criticism and hostility. One day he came in with a look of chagrin and commented, "Well, if I get one more letter commending me for statesmanship, I may need to reconsider my position!" His quip did not suggest that he does not appreciate an encouraging word, nor did it insinuate that statesmanship is not a worthy pursuit. Rather, he was reflecting on what seemed to be a lifetime of reviling and wondering why that had changed.

Jesus warned His followers to beware when others spoke well of them. In Scripture, it seems that false prophets were popular, while true prophets endured persecution.[19] True disciples of Jesus will experience persecution and false accusation. Yet they can rejoice in knowing that they are following in the steps of the prophets and moving forward to their reward in heaven.

Categories of Suffering

This Beatitude describes three categories of suffering to be endured by believers: (1) reviling, (2) persecution, and (3) defamation of character. All three words used in the text suggest ways in which the suffering would be administered, ranging from emotional outbursts of unkind words to the pressure of unrelenting pursuit to the uncertainty of unfounded threats. It was not uncommon for all to be employed at once.

"Reviling" (Greek *oneidisōsin*) is a reference to verbal abuse. Anyone who is despised and has been subjected to the assault of taunting words has entered the school of patience. To experience this verbal beating requires endurance that is possible only through the indwelling Holy Spirit. I have heard my husband say on more than one occasion, "If I believed everything I read about me in the papers, I'd hate me, too!"

I remember listening to my husband's accusers use some ambiguous words in response to his request for an unveiling of the accusations levied against him: "If you knew what we knew." The point is that my husband, who was the accused, did not know what charges were being waged against him. By all rights, he should have been among the first to receive that information.

Persecution (Greek *diōxōsin*) in its root meaning of "pursuing" expresses the idea of "harassing" or "troubling." In fact, the sense of meaning is that the world would be running after or pursuing believers in order to cause them suffering. Believers are encouraged to refrain from drawing persecution upon themselves. There will always be those who would hunt down anyone who is totally committed to the Lord.

A Grammatical Point of Interest

The verbs describing categories of suffering in the Greek text are in the aorist *tense.*[20] *This tense suggests an event that happened at a prescribed time in the past instead of an action that is ongoing and continual. In other words, the persecution does indeed happen, but it is not necessarily to be constant day in and day out. That is not to suggest that once you endure persecution you will never see it again, but it does give a window of hope for deliverance!*

The third category of suffering is defamation of character (Greek *pseudomenoi*) in the sense of "uttering an untruth" or "attempting to deceive by falsehood." This word is transliterated into English as *pseudonym,* meaning "a fictitious name," often for the purpose of concealing identity. Such is presupposed by the allusion to "threats" in 1 Peter 3:14. This type of persecution has often been administered by totalitarian states. The Christian community is sometimes subjected to compulsory measures even in the midst of its legitimate activity. What the state considers lawful is not always confined to the administration of justice.

Christians living under Communist regimes experienced the scrutiny of totalitarian atheism. They were constantly under suspicion. Their words were often distorted; facts were not considered; and their actions were considered treasonous because they were Christians. Godly pastors and committed believers were hauled into dingy interrogation rooms for no reason other than that they had assembled for fellowship and worship. They were held on the pretense of vague threats without any contact with family or friends.

The challenge is to keep the standard of righteousness high when under persecution, being certain that you are among the righteous. Righteousness means thinking what God thinks, feeling what God feels, being willing to do what God wants you to do. To live righteously is to commit your life to God each day, in any circumstance, and in every place. This makes persecution a meaningful happening because of the goal ahead, for such suffering contains the certainty of reward.[21] The Lord acknowledges as His children those who endure suffering for the sake of righteousness. For His children, there is reason to rejoice.

These Beatitudes also identify some general principles that apply to believers. First, a woman committed to Christ ought to be unlike any non-Christian woman. This difference should not be minimal, but the believer should have a different nature. The gospel of Jesus Christ creates a distinction between the believer and the unbeliever, and this division inevitably leads to the unbeliever's antagonism toward the believer.[22] Persecution is a good test for the reality and genuineness of your Christian faith.

Second, the believer's life should be controlled by Christ. She is to be governed by her loyal devotion to Him and motivated to do everything for Christ's sake. In fact, her focus in life is to live for Christ and not for herself.[23]

Third, the believer's life should be kept in check by her thoughts of heavenly reward. She thinks about what is to come. Heaven is always on her mind as a reminder of the coming fellowship with the Lord Jesus.[24]

Fourth, persecution is permitted by God for spiritual refinement.[25] There is no better measure of our spiritual growth than coming through the fire. I love fine sterling silver—flatware, serving pieces, statuary, jewelry. I have many exquisite pieces. I have learned over the years that silver requires a great deal of care. When I polish a large silver tray, I know the tray is ready for service when I can see my reflection on its surface. What an appropriate parallel to your relationship to the Lord Jesus. He will refine you through the fire of trials and tribulations, and He will do so until He can see His image in you![26]

A Woman's Wisdom

"Because we cannot see the hand of God in our affairs, we rush to the conclusion that He has lost sight of them and of us. We look at the 'seemings' of things instead of at the underlying facts, and declare that, because God is unseen, He must necessarily be absent. And especially is this the case if we are conscious of having ourselves wandered away from Him and forgotten Him. We judge Him by ourselves, and think that He must have also forgotten and forsaken us. We measure His truth by our falseness, and find it hard to believe He can be faithful when we know ourselves to be so unfaithful."

—Hannah Whitall Smith

The blessings of the Christian life are promised to those who meet Jesus' conditions. Persecution will come in many ways, but what really matters is how believers face this suffering. They are not free to retaliate. The natural instinct for self-preservation makes resistance to vengeance difficult. Believers must not harbor resentment and bitterness.[27] They must refuse to let persecution send them into depression and unhappiness so that they lose control of their Christian optimism and turn away from their trust in the Lord's faithfulness.[28]

For you to follow Christ, to think His thoughts, and to adopt His ways will put you under condemnation by those who are in opposition to Him. It is as if you are a living rebuke and perpetual source of irritation to those who reject Christ. You may be socially ostracized by acquaintances, ignored by friends, and even rejected by family.

A Woman's Wisdom

"May I adore the mystery I cannot comprehend. Help me to be not too curious in prying into those secret things that are known only to thee, O God, nor too rash in censuring what I do not understand."

—Susanna Wesley

Jesus never minimizes the difficulties of following Him. The privileges of the Christian life are always presented with a corresponding responsibility and obligation. There are always obstacles to overcome in pursuing the purposes of God for your life. Yet eternal gain will always overshadow any earthly loss. Your motives will doubtless be impugned, and any imperfections you may have will be magnified and broadcast far and wide. The world cries out for tolerance and complacency, but you have a higher challenge.[29]

During the times when my husband and I have experienced such misunderstanding and even injustice, he has kept before me a phrase that says it all: "All you have to do is please God." How right he is! You will never be able to please the world, nor can you always be popular, even in the community of believers. To please one person is often to displease another. However, when you determine to please God, you win His commendation. This is what counts![30]

When the master craftsman fashions a stringed instrument, he first attaches each string and tests the string for construction and tuning. Only after the artisan has finished his work and attached all the strings is he ready to play the strings for melodious music. God fashions the human heart for future perfection. It is as if He is tuning the strings to see how His work is progressing. The ultimate joy will come in the future.

In the first century when this sermon was delivered, believers experienced widespread physical persecution. Christians living under Roman rule often suffered to the death, and they did so in a most agonizing way. Some would be put in the arena with wild beasts and torn asunder; others would be covered with tar to become torches for their persecutors as they burned to death. Such cruel persecution has never been completely absent from the world. However, recent generations have been marked by more subtle cruelties. Perhaps the sharp tongue of criticism, the cynical laughter of slander, and the widespread damage of false accusers are hurts inflicted upon you. The maligning of character is common even among those who claim to be Christians.

The pronounced blessing of this Beatitude comes when suffering is endured because of devotion to the Lord. Those blessed have the privilege to drink of His sufferings and thus experience unique fellowship with the Savior.[31] They are blessed in a progressive sense as tribulation produces patience; patience brings experience; and experience gives birth to hope.[32] There is also an eschatological blessing as those persecuted for righteousness' sake look forward to reward in the life to come.

A Woman's Wisdom

"Dear Lord, I thank thee for all the trials, through which thou didst lead me, and by which thou didst prepare me to behold thy Glory. Thou hast never forsaken nor forgotten me."

—Katherine von Bora[33]

Leaping for Joy

In the second statement Jesus used a strong word to express the rejoicing (Greek, *chairete*). This word, from the same root as the Greek *charis*, often translated "grace" or "graciousness," suggests the godly influence upon the heart reflected in life. Joy or liberality is a natural concomitant of this. Rejoicing is to come even in the midst of persecution. In verse 12 the rejoicing is amplified with another verb that increases the intensity of joy—"be exceeding glad" (Greek *agalliasthe*, meaning "rejoice greatly" or "jump for joy").

In the Book of Revelation, these verbs are used together again in the same way to express overwhelming joy. Christ encouraged the heavenly singers to rejoice in extending an exuberant invitation and to keep on rejoicing and jumping for joy because of the arrival of the bride at the wedding of the Lamb.[34] In the same way, Christ calls His followers to rejoice in the midst of persecution because of the heavenly award they will receive. In the Gospel of Luke, a parallel text to the passage under observation here reads: "Rejoice in that day and leap for joy."[35]

A Grammatical Word of Interest

Both verbs in Matthew 5:12 are present imperatives. They are directives or commands, and their tense suggests continual action. In other words, the reference is not to a temporary joy at a particular time but to a permanent and continuous attitude of happiness. Persecution does not produce the joy, but it cannot destroy this constant and perpetual joy bubbling from within a heart committed to the Lord Jesus.

Any woman who rejoices over persecution for its own sake is missing the point. In fact, acts of persecution are a source of grief not only because of pain inflicted but also because of the effect of sin on the world and its people.

Acts of violence have now moved to businesses, homes, churches, and school yards. Tragedies are not limited to the large metropolitan areas where drugs and crime are common, but they have hit in small, intimate communities. Cassie Bernall and Rachel Scott were among those caught in a campus shooting rampage at Columbine High School in Littleton, Colorado. The headquarters of one of the largest and most influential evangelical family organizations in the world is located in the shadow of this site. I have spoken to retreats for women in this part of the state. My husband has preached in churches in the community.

On this quiet suburban campus twelve innocent teenagers and a teacher were brutally murdered by two Columbine students who then killed themselves. Cassie's mother has indicated in public testimony that her daughter's life proclaimed that it is "better to die for what you believe than to live a lie." Those who witnessed the violence and death said that the armed students asked Cassie: "Do you believe in God?"

Cassie paused but then said, "Yes." And they killed her. Those listening said that her voice was strong. Death came instantly, and the evidence showed that she had been shot in the head at close range.

Witnesses to the death of Rachel Scott shared similar testimony. The witness of these courageous girls in the bud of youthful beauty and brimming with potential has been as a shining beam of light to their peers. No doubt the Christian lifestyle they had adopted made them a target for these angry and violent young men.[36]

What then brings rejoicing? The Lord answered this question when He stated that persecution often affirms who you are in Christ. When you are persecuted for Christ's sake, you know you belong to Him! In addition, you have identified yourself with Christ as your life has become like His.[37] An eternal reward awaits you. This reward is not deserved or earned, but it comes through the channel of God's grace. You can rejoice because the accusations against you are false. You can also rejoice in knowing that the gospel will not be hindered but will prosper and accomplish what the Lord pleases.[38]

A Woman's Wisdom

"My life is consecrated to God, to suffer for Him, as well as to enjoy Him."

—Madame Jeanne Guyon

Suffering for a Purpose

These afflictions and trials come to believers because of their association with the Savior, who Himself suffered in order to provide their redemption. This suffering also brings believers into a special fellowship of godly martyrs who have gone before. Finally, persecution for Christ's sake brings reward in heaven.[39]

What if you lose everything on earth when the alternative is to gain everything in heaven![40] However, the inheritance of heaven is not to be viewed as a reward for personal merit. Rather, it is a means of testifying of your loyalty to Christ and His righteousness.[41] Suffering, for a believer, can be the fruit of genuine commitment so that it becomes a badge of true discipleship.

Enduring injustice and trials begins with the believer's commitment to the Lord and with the realization that God always has a purpose when He allows your suffering.[42] God never loses control, nor does He preside over happenstance. Whatever happens, however tragic, you can be assured that God has permitted that event. Some of the greatest blessings and opportunities in your life may come as you walk down the pathway of pain.

The apostle Paul acknowledged this truth when he alluded to his own burden, which seemed to be as a "thorn in the flesh." Concerning an apparent physical malady that continually plagued him, Paul said that God was sufficient to meet his needs even in chronic suffering.[43] Jesus Himself was made perfect through suffering as He accomplished the task of redemption through His death on the cross.[44] You must also allow God to fight your battles since He alone is to activate vengeance on your behalf.[45]

Aloma Baptist Church in Winter Park, Florida, sent some of their young people with sponsors to work in door-to-door evangelism in another part of the state. As the group returned, a tire blew out, flipping the van. One of the sponsors was killed instantly and seven others were critically injured. They suffered serious burns and internal injuries that required weeks of hospitalization. The only person who walked away from the accident was a young woman who was to leave almost immediately for Japan and a year of mission service.

These young people and the adults who accompanied them had ministered faithfully in their assignment. Who can explain why something like this would happen to such good people? Susie Rabun, whose husband died in the crash, expressed it well, "I would do it all over again for Jesus." Brian Gilliland testified, "Life is brief. Knowing that, I want to be found faithful."[46]

The Lord does not express pity and doom for those enduring persecution. Rather, He extends congratulations and commendations. Whining is not acceptable. On the other hand, the rejoicing is not because suffering in itself is good but because suffering is the fruit of righteous living. You could even consider persecution and suffering a *visible* token of genuine Christian commitment.[47]

A Woman's Wisdom

"As iron is fashioned by fire and on an anvil, so in the fire of suffering and under the weight of trials, our souls receive the form which our Lord desires them to have."

—St. Madeleine Sophie Barat

Every person who endures suffering is not a believer deserving of reward or even a believer. The heavenly reward is reserved for those whose suffering is *for the sake of righteousness.* A person who reaches for martyrdom is not to be praised.

Persecution, however, can be a path to spiritual growth as the difficulties and challenges of life are met and overcome through the Lord's grace and strength.[48] How often believers have passed through suffering and sorrow only to find that to experience the Lord's assurance and comfort is worth it all.

Jon and Sherry Walker have done this "pass through" more than once. Their most recent journey of suffering involved the loss of Jeremy, the baby whom Sherry carried in her womb for thirty-four weeks. Jeremy was a victim of Trisomy 18 and spina bifida; he died during birth. According to his loving father, Jeremy's legs were "brutally crumpled," but the winsome baby was complete with fingers, toes, and ruddy complexion. Sherry has lost four babies over the years. Yet, she and Jon do not dwell on the losses but rejoice in the daily grace God gives as He uses even the dark hours to accomplish His purposes in the lives of His children.

The Walkers have been blessed with one healthy son. Christopher brightens their home with his happy spirit, reminding them of the Father's gracious mercy in their lives. In one of Jon's editorials for *HomeLife* magazine, he quoted the British philosopher C. S. Lewis: "I know now, Lord, why you utter no answer. You are yourself the answer. Before your face questions die away." Yes, for the Walkers and for you, God's presence is the answer.[49]

The rose is an enigma, and it often provokes contradictory responses. If you cut a rose and prick your finger, you may complain that roses have thorns; and they do! On the other hand, even with a pricked finger, you must be grateful that in the midst of all those thorns is one of the most beautiful and fragrant flowers God ever made.

Roses often grow in profusion, and this results in some wonderful by-products. The roses are harvested and their petals stripped off. Those petals are compressed to produce rare and fragrant rose water. I love to spray this delicate fragrance throughout our home or pour it over my hands and splash it on my face or use it to scent my linens.

The fields of roses are beautiful and fragrant, but they do not have the lasting fragrance of the rose water, which, in turn, comes only when the pressure is so overwhelming and heavy that the petals are reduced to liquid. The pressure and crushing in your life is a necessary prelude to achieve the long-lasting fragrance that comes out of great suffering. This fragrance comes from Jesus, the everlasting Rose of Sharon, and the power of His fragrance permeates beyond any other.[50]

A Woman's Wisdom

"I know that these contradictory events are permitted and guided by thy wisdom, which solely is light. We are in darkness and must be thankful that our knowledge is not wanted [needed] to perfect thy work."

—St. Elizabeth Seton

History reveals that the church of the Lord Jesus Christ has experienced some of its greatest evangelistic outreach and growth during times of persecution. In the dark hours, the Lord comes alongside to provide comforting grace, and usually a believer is more ready to enjoy this intimate fellowship. Not only do Christians grow through such experiences, but the church also is purged of pseudo-believers who are not willing to pay the cost of discipleship.[51] The call of Christ is not primarily a call to enjoy happiness and prosperity but a challenge to bear up under difficulties and to endure hardship.

Steve and Stacy Marshall found themselves lying on a dirty bathroom floor in a northern Cambodian hotel. The sounds of fighting were all around them; their accommodations were less than adequate; their food was scarce and not very appetizing; they were scared to death. Up to that point, they had not seen many conversions, and they wanted to go home. They found themselves crying and praying as the rockets hit across the street, lighting up the darkness, Steve remembers: "We drew a 'faith line' for ourselves."

The Marshalls had the opportunity to evacuate the next day because of the inherent dangers in their location. But they counted the cost and decided to step across that "faith line" and place themselves under the protection of the Lord to complete their assignment of sharing the love of Christ with a gospel-resistant people.

They were not prepared for the results of this step of faith. The Cambodians were overwhelmed with the courage of this young couple. These people had never been open to the gospel. Yet suddenly, Steve and Stacy began to see as many as forty-five conversions in a day! God opened the windows of heaven and poured out His blessings. Yes, they returned safely—and bearing precious sheaves in the harvest of souls won to Christ.[52]

The Power of Suffering

Suffering also has the potential to open doors to wider usefulness in the kingdom because your intimacy with the Lord will drive you to purity of life. It is no accident that the greatest spiritual awakenings have begun with a few spiritually sensitive believers rather than with the masses of Christendom.

A Woman's Wisdom

"I trust in the same powerful God, that his holy arm and power will carry me through, whatever he hath yet for me to do. . . . I know his faithfulness and goodness, and I have experienced his love."

—Margaret Fell Fox

Suffering offers the potential for testimony that surpasses all others. Remember the first-century believers who were literally swept to the ends of the earth by persecution from both the Jewish hierarchy and the government of Rome. They were scattered abroad and in their flight, they "went everywhere preaching the Word."[53] They literally set the world on fire with their evangelistic fervor and the testimonies of their faith.[54]

Such commitment did not end in the first century. Ann Hasseltine Judson literally sacrificed her own life in trying to reach Burma for

Christ. She walked away from a comfortable and affluent home. She
buried her children on foreign soil. She ministered to her husband
Adoniram as he languished in prison. Ann testified: "I am a creature of
God, and he has an undoubted right to do with me as seemeth good in
his sight. I rejoice that I am in his hand—that he is everywhere present
and can protect me in one place as well as in another."[55]

Divine grace has enabled women who have been maligned, misunderstood, and oppressed to receive comfort and strength from the
Lord. Consider the woman who came to the house of Simon the
Pharisee with humility and penitence seeking the Savior's forgiveness,[56]
Mary of Bethany who sat at Jesus' feet eager to learn more of Him,[57]
and Mary Magdalene who with loving loyalty went to His tomb.[58] These
women experienced ridicule and rebuke as they sought to worship the
Savior. Jesus experienced ridicule when He should have had loving
support;[59] He endured suspicion when He should have had committed
cooperation;[60] He felt censure when there should have been encouragement.[61] Even His family became His foes on occasion.[62] His own
mother misunderstood Him.[63]

The history of the church has demonstrated that persecution will
come upon Christians. Perpetua, a native of Carthage, was a young
widow in the early church.[64] She was ordered to offer sacrifices to the
emperor of Rome. Her family encouraged her to recant her faith since
she was facing certain death. She chose to remain firm. Perpetua,
together with her slave Felicitas, was subjected to flogging, exposed to
wild animals, and finally beheaded in the Carthage arena.

The testimony from the pen of this martyr remains a light for
women who have followed in her steps in unwavering commitment to
Christ. Perpetua wrote, "What I now suffer, I suffer myself; but then
there will be Another who will suffer with me, because I also shall suffer for Him." There have been women all through history who have
been willing to dedicate themselves in unfaltering devotion to Christ,
even at the cost of their lives.

Conclusion

Persecution may be marked with raging fiery trials, but remember that fire cleanses metal of its dross. The refining process brings beauty and usefulness. The sculptor's chisel strips away rough exteriors and fashions shapeless stone to beauty and worth. Jesus sent His disciples into the world to minister to people and to carry the gospel. He did not send them into cloistered existence in monasteries or convents.

A Woman's Wisdom

"Melancholy is the poison of devotion. When one is in tribulation, it is necessary to be more happy and more joyful because one is nearer to God."

—Clare of Assisi

The Lord chose to place this Beatitude on persecution at the end of the list. Perhaps He wanted the blessings and rewards for following Christ to be very apparent before the costly price was clearly put forth. Jesus also extended His message beyond the inner circle of followers who were already in the midst of persecution. He concluded by making it clear that persecution does not take away from the blessings of righteous living but rather adds to those blessings. Salvation is past, present, and future. It is first received as the gift of God and then is enjoyed in the present through God's faithfulness only to reach its climactic eschatological reward in the life to come.

A Grammatical Note

By using the more impersonal third person pronoun "theirs" in Matthew 5:10, the Lord reached out to all who were listening to His sermon on the mountain as well. His message about the requirements for blessing and the cost of discipleship was also available for the generations to follow, for any person who would receive its message.

Victory follows the battle; the crown comes after the cross. Life comes after death; rest follows labor. Without His suffering, there would be no eternal rest; without His death, you would not have life eternal. Jesus wants to help you face the ordinary duties of life with a heart totally committed to Him. He has promised His help and all-sufficient grace to believers who are facing trials and tribulations for His sake.

Fanny Crosby, who wrote the lyrics for eight thousand hymns, lost her eyesight as an infant because of the negligence of a doctor who came to treat her in the absence of the family physician.[65] Once the consequences were apparent, the careless man left town and was never heard from again. Typical of Crosby was the testimony she shared during her eighty-fifth year. She affirmed her forgiveness of the negligent physician who robbed her of eyesight and expressed her contentment with the circumstances of her life.

A Woman's Wisdom

My song shall be of Jesus.
When sitting at his feet,
I call to mind his goodness
And know my joy's complete.
My song shall be of Jesus.
Whatever ills befall,
I'll sing the grace that saves me,
And triumphs over all.

—Fanny J. Crosby

Sightless and dependent on others, Crosby was well aware of inevitable stumbling and continual uncertainties. She understood as few others what it meant to trust the Lord to guide her steps and give the necessary grace to walk through the hard places and overcome the obstacles of life. The basis for her happiness in the midst of adversity was her confidence that the Lord had consecrated her for the work of writing hymns and had equipped her with all she needed to do the sacred task!

Prayer and Meditation

Father, how easy it is to love You and do Your work when we have no troubles and enjoy happy times! But how much more rewarding it is to know that we love You, not for special privileges to be attained or for continued prosperity to be enjoyed, but rather just because of who You are and what You have done in giving Your life for our salvation. Whether in difficulties or trials, whether in sickness or health, whether in poverty or wealth, Lord Jesus, draw us within the circle of Your loving care. We would choose to be victors, not victims; we would determine to be overcomers, not those who give up; we want to be forgivers of wrongdoing and not bookkeepers on evil; we want to be like You! *We affirm with the hymn writer,*

> *When darkness seems to hide His face,*
> *I rest on His unchanging grace;*
> *In ev'ry high and stormy gale,*
> *My anchor holds within the veil.*
> *On Christ, the solid Rock, I stand;*
> *All other ground is sinking sand,*
> *All other ground is sinking sand.*[66]

—Edward Mote

Moments for Enrichment

A VERSE TO MEMORIZE

"But when you do good and suffer for it, if you take it patiently, this is commendable before God. For to this you were called, because Christ also suffered for us, leaving us an example, that you should follow His steps" (1 Pet. 2:20b–21).

ACTIVITIES TO ENHANCE YOUR UNDERSTANDING OF THE TEXT:

1. Consider the course of suffering in your own life—when, where, and how it came. The accompanying chart may be a tool for determining how God has guided you through the challenges of your life.

Event of Suffering	Deliverance	Biblical Hope
1. Miscarriage	Reunion with child in heaven	2 Sam. 12:23
2. Chronic pain	God's presence within	Isa. 41:10
3. Slander	God settles the account	Matt. 12:36–37
4.		
5.		

2. Theologians use the term *theodicy* to describe the interaction of divine providence with evil. There are no easy answers to the question of why bad things happen to good people. The accompanying chart is a tool to record how God has brought good out of evil in the lives of women in the Bible. He can do the same in your life.

A Godly Person	Suffered Evil	Won Victory
1. Naaman's maid servant	Forced into slavery	Responsible for introducing Syrian general to the God of Israel
2. Esther	Taken into pagan harem of cruel monarch	Saved God's people from destruction
3. Anna	Widowed at early age	Held infant Messiah in the temple
4.		
5.		

3. In your own quiet time meditate and record what resources you can claim when suffering comes.

The Kind of Suffering	God's Promise
1. Loneliness	1 John 1:3, 7
2. Fear	Josh. 1:9
3. Pain	Isa. 41:10
4. Sorrow	Isa. 60:20
5.	
6.	

4. Perhaps you would learn some valuable lessons in how to deal with your own suffering by looking at the lives of Bible women who suffered.

Bible Woman	How She Suffered	How She Overcame
1. Hannah	Barrenness	Prayer
2. Abigail	Abusive husband	Doing what she could
3.		
4.		

Notes

1. John 16:13.
2. Matt. 5:3–9.
3. John 1:10.
4. Matt. 10:22.
5. John 15:18–20.
6. 1 Sam. 1:5–7, 15–18.
7. 1 Sam. 1:19–20; 3:19–20.
8. 2 Kings 5:1–14.
9. Exod. 1:15–21.
10. Isa. 43:2–3.
11. Rom. 12:1–2.
12. Acts 6:8, 15; 7:55.
13. Matt. 5:14–16.
14. Matt. 21:12–13.
15. Acts 19:23–41.
16. John 15:18–21; 1 Pet. 4:12–14.
17. Luke 6:26.
18. John 1:10; 15:18–19; 17:16.
19. Matt. 7:15; 24:11, 24.
20. Matt. 5:11.
21. Rev. 2:10.
22. Gal. 5:17–21.
23. Gal. 2:20; Col. 1:27.
24. John 14:1–4.
25. Mal. 3:3.
26. Ps. 66:10.
27. Heb. 12:14–15.
28. Ps. 37:3–4.
29. Phil. 3:14.
30. 2 Tim. 4:7–8.
31. Phil. 3:10.
32. Rom. 5:3–5.

33. Katie, who lived during the sixteenth century, suffered at the hands of the established church as did her husband. The great Reformer Martin Luther was the catalyst for opening the door to the free-church movement across Europe.

34. Rev. 19:7.

35. Luke 6:22–23.

36. Assorted releases from Baptist Press, Spring 1999.

37. 2 Cor. 5:17–18.

38. Isa. 55:11.

39. Acts 5:41; Rom. 8:17.

40. Matt. 6:19–21.

41. Acts 5:41–42.

42. John 19:11.

43. 2 Cor. 12:9–10.

44. Heb. 2:10.

45. Deut. 32:35.

46. Baptist Press release transcript by Shari Schubert, 27 August 1999.

47. Matt. 5:12.

48. 2 Cor. 12:9.

49. Personal correspondence with Jon Walker, editor of *HomeLife* magazine, 1999.

50. See Song of Sol. 2:1; 2 Cor. 2:15.

51. Matt. 16:24–25.

52. Ps. 126:5–6.

53. Acts 8:4.

54. Rev. 12:11.

55. She lived from 1789 to 1826.

56. Luke 7:36–50.

57. John 11:1–2.

58. John 20:11–18.

59. Luke 23:35–39.

60. Luke 5:17–26.

61. Luke 6:6–11.

62. Luke 8:19–21.

63. John 2:1–11.

64. She lived c. 180–203.

65. Crosby lived from 1820 to 1915.

66. Edward Mote, "The Solid Rock," 1863.

Conclusion

An Addendum on
Personal Happiness

The question remains: Can a woman find genuine happiness and lasting prosperity? The spiritual pilgrimage set forth in the Beatitudes is before you for consideration. The text has been read and explained and applied. The climactic paradox[1] is the most amazing of all! If you do succeed in living this set-apart life based on the principles taught by Jesus in this classic sermon, you *will* be persecuted. What a reward for a job well done!

Although the concept of living righteously and being persecuted may seem to be a contradiction, it makes perfect sense. The more you succeed in being like Jesus, the more the world will treat you as they treated Him. The gospel does offer comfort to the afflicted, but it also has a way of afflicting the comfortable!

A personal anecdote provides a vignette of genuine happiness. In February 1992, I sat in the Admiral's Club of the busy Dallas/Fort Worth Airport in the midst of enjoying a moment of happiness. My husband and I had just come from Richmond, Virginia. While there we received a telephone call from Mark Howell requesting an appointment with us. This young preacher had been dating our daughter Carmen for over a year. For several weeks their mutual love for each other and desire to link their lives together in marital commitment had been apparent.

Carmen would receive her degree in biblical studies in May, and Mark was finishing his seminary M.Div. with plans to enter a Ph.D. program. Mark arrived in Dallas early enough for a secret rendezvous with my husband and me to discuss future plans for Carmen and him. We talked and prayed together. Mark expressed his love for Carmen and his desire to make her his wife and colaborer in all that God would give them to do in the kingdom.

My husband had long bragged about making any young man seeking the hand of his only daughter "sweat out" a lengthy interrogation. But even the Big Daddy was so overcome with the happiness of the moment that the grueling questions he had prepared became encouraging affirmations instead. My husband and I gave our happy consent—yes, our joyous affirmation of God's direction for Carmen and Mark.

The next time our daughter and her beloved appeared, Carmen's eyes matched the sparkle of a beautiful diamond on her finger. She was officially engaged. My prayers concerning the future of our only daughter had been answered far above and beyond what I had dared to ask of the Lord. However, leading up to this supreme moment of happiness were many contrasting experiences. Carmen always dated fine Christian young men, but her dating experiences had been marked by highs and lows. Often someone infatuated with her did not awaken her interest, or occasionally her feelings for someone were not reciprocated.

Yes, in every aspect of Carmen's life, as in yours, there have been happy moments interlaced with times of great despair. Perhaps most unsettling in such a scenario is the vast range of contrasts—the high and low, the good and bad, the certain and uncertain. Isn't that typical of the path to happiness!

Some Concluding Thoughts on Happiness

Life cannot be planned to include only happy times.
Happiness, like beauty, is actually enhanced by contrast. Neither
Carmen and Mark nor her dad and I would have enjoyed the pinnacle
of happiness that came at the time of her engagement without a frame
of reference that included the contrasting feelings of rejection and
frustration with which to compare that ultimate happiness. Rather, our
happiness had been enriched and enhanced as it passed through the
difficulties and trials along the way. Just as momentary pleasures may
open the door to enduring pain, eternal happiness is behind the door
of ongoing testing and trials.

*Happiness must be the resulting fruit but not the ultimate
goal.* The world appears to consider happiness as the ultimate goal in
life. It defines happiness as freedom from all distress and enjoyment
of all pleasures. This is certainly not a biblical concept. Scripture
makes it clear that every person has a reason for his or her existence
and a specific assignment to complete on earth. If contentment is the
ultimate goal, you should negotiate with the cows to take over their
pastures. Their contentment with grazing in a grassy meadow seems
to overshadow the satisfaction of most human beings with their life
situations.

The English word *happy* comes from the root *hap*, which means
"chance." Unfortunately, when something "happens" to you, the first
thought is generally that the event or "happening" came by chance,
suggesting that "happiness" or the "happenings" of life occur because
of the influences of the outside world. From God's view, the world can
neither give nor deprive you of genuine happiness or joy.[2] If your joy is
dependent upon the outside world's effect upon you, then Christ
within would no longer be sufficient.

Changes that begin on the outside and move inside are beginning
at the wrong end. Jesus calls for you to start on the inside in the heart
and then to work out toward the living of life.[3] You will possess the

kingdom because you already have been possessed by the kingdom. What a deal!

Naomi had to learn this painful lesson in her search for happiness. She tried moving to new surroundings, keeping a stiff upper lip, shaking her fist at God, hosting her own pity party. Finally she decided to trust the providence of God. However, before reaching that point, she returned to Bethlehem from Moab, bereft of her sons as well as her husband, complaining that God had dealt "very bitterly" with her. In the same breath Naomi identified God as "Almighty" (Hebrew, *Shaddai*).[4]

What a paradox for Naomi to attribute her tragedies to One whom she had already acknowledged as *Shaddai* or to be "all-sufficient"! Without realizing it, she was bearing testimony to the fact that God must be trusted "for better or worse."[5] Either the Lord is fully satisfying, or He cannot satisfy at all. Jesus viewed His crucifixion day, even with its suffering and humiliation, as His coronation day because through His death He gained victory over the grave.[6]

Accidents in your life become providential appointments between you and God. Dr. Roland V. Bingham, founder of the Sudan Interior Mission, after being seriously injured in an automobile collision, said that there were no accidents in the life of a Christian—only incidents through which God works. Even when outward conditions do not correspond to the desired good, this blessedness exists inwardly through the gift of grace and enjoyment of fellowship with God.

Herman Cremer described blessedness as "the life-joy and satisfaction of the man [or woman] who does or shall experience God's favor and salvation, his blessedness altogether apart from his outward condition." This blessedness is dependent upon your living in harmony with God and not upon your being on good terms with everyone else at the sacrifice of godly principles. A woman who is so blessed views what the world calls *disappointments* as being God's *appointments* for her life, and she is satisfied to accept those appointments as they come.

"Disappointment—His appointment,"
Change one letter, then I see
That the thwarting of my purpose
Is God's better choice for me.
His appointment must be blessing,
Tho' it may come in disguise,
For the end from the beginning
Open to His wisdom lies.

"Disappointment—His appointment,"
"No good will He withhold";
From denials oft we gather
Treasures of His love untold.
Well He knows each broken purpose
Leads to fuller, deeper trust,
And the end of all His dealings
Proves our God is wise and just.

"Disappointment—His appointment,"
Lord, I take it, then, as such,
Like the clay in hands of potter,
Yielding wholly to Thy touch.
All my life's plan is Thy molding,
Not one single choice be mine;
Let me answer, unrepining—
"Father, not my will, but Thine."⁷

Happiness is only the bridesmaid and not the bride. My
thoughts still return on occasion to memories of the beautiful and
meaningful wedding of our daughter to her beloved in the summer of
1992. However, through the years the happy memories of careful planning and meticulous preparation for the wedding event have been
overshadowed by the living reality of the maturation of love between

Mark and Carmen and by their faithfulness in commitment to each other within an enduring marriage.

Jesus continually seeks to communicate with ordinary, simple people like you and me.[8] Yet the Sermon on the Mount forces you to acknowledge that there is a great distance between the Lord God and His creation. It is never easy to teach heavenly lessons; yet you must constantly seek to reduce the distance between God and you. Jesus never lowered God's standard, but He graciously offers His grace to bridge the gap between God and sinful human beings. Your goal is to strive to be like Him.

To follow Christ is to determine to be like Him, and to be like Him is to go against the tide. You must move beyond merely being forgiven and pursue holiness and spiritual growth with enthusiasm. It's the inside that needs transformation! Only love for and commitment to Jesus Christ will make you His disciple and drive you to learn to be like Him so that the natural outflow of your life will be a determination to please Him.

Genuine faith leads to discipleship and transformation of life. The believing woman who would follow Christ and seek to be like Him must assume responsibility for molding her life in the mold He provides. If you would have the heart and mind of Christ, you must follow Him aggressively in the practices of daily living. Passivity is the curse of the modern era. In the spiritual realm there is no room for complacency or merely letting it happen. The Beatitudes are not about passively receiving the blessings that come with belonging to Him. Rather, they are a challenge to actively pursuing a life dedicated to Him.

The challenge for you in making the appropriation of these "BeAttitudes" a priority in your life begins with a divine appointment in which you are willing to acknowledge God not only as the Creator of the universe but also as the Lord who must be obeyed. You then seek your happiness in all the right places. Whatever your circumstances or disappointments, you can be confident that it is not a happenstance but a *chosen commitment* that produces genuine happiness.

Notes

1. Matt. 5:10–12.
2. John 16:22; see also Prov. 23:7.
3. Luke 12:34.
4. *Shaddai* suggests the sense of "all sufficiency" (see Ruth 1:20–21).
5. See Prov. 24:10.
6. 1 Cor. 15:51–56.
7. Spiros Zodhiates, *The Pursuit of Happiness* (Grand Rapids: Wm. B. Eerdmans, 1960), 20–21.
8. Isa. 40:5.